The
Happiness Warrior

Finding Your
Instinctive-Self
Within
Western Civilization

By
Dr. Clare Hinsley

ISBN: 978-1-913012-36-6

Published in partnership with Riverside Publishing Solutions.

Printed and bound in the UK by Severn, Gloucester

Acknowledgements

I would like to express my deepest gratitude to my partner for his support which has enabled me to follow my calling on this journey. My children have been extremely supportive through their growing independence and their positive outlook on life.

Although distance separates us, my parents, sisters, and their families have all provided encouraging support and care towards my health throughout this process. These beautiful individuals have made this book possible.

My research has coincided with an engineering career of which I am fortunate to have such wonderful colleagues who patiently listened to my concepts. For their listening ears, I give great thanks.

I owe a deeper understanding of Metaphysics to Dr. Masters and all of his staff at the University of Metaphysics and the University of Sedona for their support and dedication to enlightening all those who are interested.

Acknowledgements

Lastly, I would like to thank the daily opportunities which enable me to practice the abilities discussed in this book and yourself for reading it. May each of you personally bridge the gap between spirituality and science through your own experiences.

I dedicate this book
to my parents
for without their love
I would be without form

Contents

Introduction

A connection to our instinctive-Self exists within all of us. Throughout my life this connection has shown itself many times, although it wasn't until recent years I lost the fear of hiding from it and began embracing it. Through much effort, I found peace within and I endeavour to simplify this process for others.

Those who read these words, may you realise that you are truly blessed and peace *WILL* come to you. It just requires effort and faith on your part. The power to create a better life resides within each and every one of us.

Our purpose in life is to evolve. For plants, evolving is to grow bigger and in many cases producing flowers. Human evolvement is a spiritual journey back to the Creator. We all know this inside, but instead we have been taught to think that money is the key. If money was the key, why are not all billionaires ecstatically happy? The happiest people seem to be the ones who don't connect with money, look at children for example. The less they know about money, the more they run around playing and enjoying themselves. Shamans, Buddha's and Mystics seem also to be carefree. The less they care about money, the more at peace they are within themselves. Those who have connections with the Creator do enjoy life more than those who limit themselves with items of form.

The foundation of Metaphysics is to experience things on a personal level. Anyone can go to a library and find millions of books full of information. Unfortunately, this information is rendered useless until someone picks up one of the books and begins reading it. At this point the information is still just information until the reader applies it to their own existence. By combining scientific facts with a selection of philosophies, this book makes concepts easier to accept as well as thought provoking. My goal is for others to question everything until they understand who they are and what everything means to them personally.

Some call human evolvement the Ascension process. Others call it finding God, connecting to Source Energy, or even living life more instinctively. Whatever you choose to call it, this process is something that can be achieved by anyone. Once achieved, life becomes filled with excitement, Inner Peace, and happiness. The stresses and strains of life become comical and take on

Introduction

the form of direction markers rather than manifesting negative physical symptoms. There are many sources of information about this process, but the majority seem to lack instruction. This leaves a person wanting to ascend but not knowing where to start. Of course there is no pill one can take to wake up the next morning and see everything in a more positive way. It is a process, a process that one must undertake. It requires effort. I don't know anyone who can pick up a guitar for the first time and expect to play to concert standards. In this book I will lay out the steps and exercises which will enable your own Inner Peace to flourish. The more effort one puts towards the exercises, the quicker one will achieve Inner Peace; it *IS* entirely under your control.

"A sorcerer asks the question, 'If we are going to die with the totality of ourselves, why not, then, live with that totality" (Castaneda, p. 131)? When life is not lived to its full potential it becomes wasted. With the knowledge of how to change your perspective, life becomes much more enjoyable, productive, and creative. In order to live life to the full, it requires increased moments of acknowledging where you are in the present moment. The more present you become, the more consciously you choose actions and reactions. Don Juan said that "the condition of a warrior is to be aware of everything at all times" (Castaneda, p. 117). Here I endeavour to teach the skills to acquire a connection with your true, instinctive-Self, through becoming more present, turning you into a warrior. Just by becoming aware of the information received from our senses, it is possible to notice the positive effect it has on our lives. Once this awareness is achieved, choices and reactions can be made from our instinctive, True-Self. This is *THE* prominent step moving towards a purer state of living. The reward gained is having the capability of picking apart the negative aspects of life until they become so diluted that they have no influence over us. I will introduce your own environmental-Self and show how it has formed as well as how it has contaminated our senses. With conscious effort, it is possible to redirect our misguided use of the senses to activate light meditational states. Through an explanation of how our sensing abilities are different to animals, I will demonstrate how to achieve the gift of experiencing higher states of consciousness.

The necessity in finding my own Inner Peace began when I found myself becoming physically ill through the stresses and strains of Western life. It was then that I started asking myself questions like "Where is my Inner Peace? Why is life so difficult?" At first these

Introduction

questions were contained within my own mind until they became frustratingly unanswered and I began voicing them. Once, while searching through papers at work, someone helpfully asked "What are you looking for?" My response was "Inner peace, I am looking for Inner peace, have you felt it?" The reaction of others was always the same, "If you find Inner Peace, can you give some to me, please?" This feedback told me that very few people living in Western Civilization are at peace within themselves. We are all very similar in the way that we are unsatisfied with our lives, our physical bodies, our jobs; we are always striving to have more money, a better car, and more appreciation. Why is this so? These questions led me to research the reasons behind this lack of satisfaction and I found that the basis lies with the way we have been taught. We live an external life rather than an internal life. We have been conditioned, throughout our whole lives, that what needs fixing is things around us, outside of us. We have been taught that happiness comes from consuming material goods. Schools do not teach children the value of being at peace within their own bodies, instead they teach lessons on history, maths and flood our minds with information that has little influence over our happiness.

In order to find Inner Peace and lead happy lives we need to fix the things within us. We need to learn how our perception has been tainted, how we have become overly and unnecessarily judgemental. There is a transformation required to sustain Inner Peace, it is a process we must go through. Our whole lives, our inner truth has been hidden from us. Luckily it can never be lost; instead it is inactive and waiting to surface. We have been distracted with information and if you continue reading this book, your inner truth will begin to shine through. Here you will find the keys to unlock your own happiness, but it is up to you to unlock the door by practicing the techniques provided. This is why the book is entitled 'The Happiness Warrior', as you will find yourself gaining a warrior-like attitude as you begin to evolve into your True-Self and shed the falsities that have been acquired throughout your lifetime.

My reason for writing this book is to support the reader on their own journey to find Inner Peace. My personal journey was very much a secretive one. I often hid my tears due to a frustration with myself and the world around me. I was so desperate to find Inner Peace that I found myself in some type of a dream state, in 2014, where my mind and body felt as though they were numb. I was aware of what was going on around me, although I felt completely detached from my environment. It was as if a positive path was illuminated before me, so much so that I had no awareness of any alternate negative paths. My perception of everything transformed completely. This process increased my confidence to the point where I turned my life upside down. I found myself committing to positive decisions that would alter my life forever, for the better!

I started by making small decisions for myself, focusing on little improvements to my own life and understanding what really mattered to me. I stripped all things from my environment that I didn't believe served me. I stopped rushing around, forcing myself to carry out activities that I used to believe were necessary. My circle of friends changed, my eating habits changed, and I transitioned myself into a simpler lifestyle.

A few years later I stumbled upon Metaphysics, and began researching the works of Dr. Paul Leon Masters, Swami Vivekananda, and C.G. Jung, to name a few. Through my studies I began meditating and found a connection with my Higher-Self which has helped to increase Inner Peace and happiness in my life.

Vivekananda, in his book *The Four Paths of Yoga*, says that "every thought and word that weakens you in this world is the only evil that exists" (p. 138). He states that "I am responsible for my fate, I am the bringer of good unto myself, I am the bringer of evil" (p. 113). It is us alone that contain the ability to conquer our own thoughts and the more we practice, the better we get at it. We are responsible for our own lives and we need to take back that responsibility and stop blaming external situations.

In this book I will discuss how, those within the Western Civilization can utilise conscious questioning (of thoughts) in order to learn the difference between one's environmental-Self and Higher-Self. It is imperative that we differentiate between our True, Higher-Self and the effects that Western Civilization has had on our egoic environmental-Self. Once it is understood how manipulating our environment potentially is, we can unravel the layers of falsities that have been engrained within our personal ego. There are so many opportunities for personal growth surrounding us, yet most of us are unaware of them. Our senses pick up information from our environment; this information is then compiled as memories and contributes as a major influence on our personality or ego. But this accumulation of memories is only a part of our makeup, not the totality of who we fully are. With the support of research, I will reveal that a connection with one's

Introduction

Higher-Self will bring Inner Peace and happiness. I will discuss different ways this connection can be achieved so as to enable as many people as possible to improve their own lives. I would like to express the positive impact this knowledge has brought to my own life and leave you with the desire to manifest the strength to do the same and improve your own life.

To find Inner-Peace rebellion is not required, just the curiosity to find out who we really are, on the inside. I welcome you to the beginning of your happier life and instil a warrior power within you to continue this journey.

The Universe is ready to fight for you and the power of the Creator is within you. Anything you focus on can be yours.

"Inspiration is believed to come from the outside, while this knowledge comes from the man himself".

∞ (Vivekananda, p. 242) ∞

Trusting Yourself

So how did we fall into living a life where we don't trust ourselves? In his book *Beyond 2012*, Wes Penre talks about how a repetitive cycle is formed where children "...grow up, go to school, and learn similar things that their parents learned..." (p. 82). Yes our parent's instilled values within us; they taught us what was right and wrong, just as their parents had taught them. But did *they* lead a life full of happiness; did *they* work towards the evolution of mankind? Did *they* take great pleasure in everything attempted or were they only happy for fleeting moments? Were *they* able to spend time with the ones they loved on their days off? Have we been taught how to be our best selves or have we just been taught to be like our parents and their parents?

Becoming a good slave has been the purpose of life for many generations as we have all been convinced that rebellious behaviour leads to the risk of losing everything without pay or employment. What happens when we fight for what is right, is this also considered rebellious behaviour? A fear has been instilled within the minds of those in Western Civilization from birth, for many generations. This fear compels us to believe that we are fighting for our survival. That it is us against the world. So we find ourselves "...exhausted from a life as a slave ... [where] you have no energy to rebel" (Penre, p. 82).

We trusted our parents, our teachers, and our employers. But what we have learned from them are only individual opinions. What makes one person happy doesn't necessarily make another person happy. We believe that trust is a difficult thing to gain, in some cases. Although in many cases trust is all too easily handed out. We will further explore how, who, and what we can trust in later chapters. The point I would like to focus on here is the fact that many of us have lost trust in ourselves. We rely so much on others telling us what to do, when to do it, even where to do it, that our abilities to trust in ourselves have become diminished. It is important to understand that our gut feelings *ARE* our most reliable guide towards living a happier life. The main hurdle then becomes distinguishing between our gut feelings and our own, so-called, rational thoughts.

There seems to be two types of people in the world. Those that breeze through life, have everything they want and others who continuously struggle encountering never-ending obstacles. Believe it or not, the lucky people also need to work very hard for what they achieve, and only a small percentage of them have managed to leave behind the troubles and strife that seem to set the majority back.

Each and every person has a soul and that soul is watching over us. Imagine looking out of a third floor window and seeing an unaided, young child cross a busy road. The vantage point from the high window makes it possible to see the traffic and any danger approaching, in both directions. The young child, however, has a completely different view from the roadside, restricted by parked cars, their own height, as well as little understanding of predicting how the traffic speeds up and slows down.

What would you do if you noticed a speeding motorcycle ducking and diving through the traffic towards the child as the child started to cross the street? A feeling of panic may rush through you and your instincts may take over in an attempt to bang on the window, or open it in order to yell warnings to the child. But what if the noise outside was so loud that you knew there was no chance to alert the child to danger? This situation would more than likely provide a sinking feeling in your stomach with the realisation that all you could do was observe the situation while having no persuasive powers over it.

This situation is very similar to how our soul views and reacts to our own individual choices and reactions. The communication is there, our soul is shouting out to us, to warn and guide us. Unfortunately we have just become so distracted by the noise of our environment that we are unable to comprehend the methods of communication. It is as though the traffic outside is so loud that we are unable to hear the warnings and advice that our own soul is screaming at us.

As impossible as it may seem, to communicate with our soul is not as difficult as we believe it to be. Those who seem to breeze through life have learned how to listen to their gut feelings, how to take advice and guidance from their soul. There are many reasons why we have lost this ability, but before we go into them we must start with the basics.

As our soul is individual to us, it must have only the best intentions for us. It would never want to hurt us; it only wants us to be happy. We have faith in many things. We have faith that the sun will come up in the morning and go down in the evening. When we go to the grocery store, we believe there will be food on the shelves. We may even trust in religious figures. As a child, we trusted our parents and elders who taught us valuable lessons. Throughout our lifetime teachers have taught us information that we trusted to be the truth. Society taught us that we must focus on building a career. We trusted that hard work leads to a lucrative career which would bring us happiness. All this time, we have been relying on what other people have told us to do to achieve happiness. Can you see how we have been taught to listen to others and ignore our own instincts?

It seems that the majority only consciously focus on one day a year to allow happiness to flow through them. That day would be our own birthday. But what is different on our birthday to any other day? What actually happens on that particular day to enable us to enjoy it more? It may be the only day a year when we decide that we *will* be happy, this may be because we make the decisions of what to do, where we want go, and take control of our actions. Carte' Diem means seize the day. Our birthday is no more special than any other day except for the fact that we have consciously decided to be happy. Of course life has a way of presenting situations that may challenge us, but none the less we tend to have more awareness, more presence, more of a determination to enjoy every minute of that particular day. We want to make the most of that day so we savour every minute. We trust in the decisions we make that day as our underlying goal is to enjoy it. After this special day and the bulk of the following days, we go back into auto-pilot mode and plod along life following other people's orders, waiting for the next big day to happen. Our focus begins to creep back to the past and/ or the future rather than the present moments.

Let us begin to trust ourselves by noting down what makes us happy. Here is space to note down three things that make you happy. After each thing that makes you happy note why this thing make you happy.

What makes me happy?

1)_____

_____

_____

_____Why?_____

_____

_____

_____

2)_____

_____

_____

_____Why?_____

_____

_____

_____

3)_____

_____

_____

_____Why?_____

_____

_____

_____

Review the three things you have written and question if they are related to material things. Are all three related to material things, or none them? Does buying a new car or buying jewellery make you happy? If so, you will probably find that the happiness gained only lasts for short periods of time. Are the things you wrote more about events such as child birth? Child birth can be a very painful experience, yet the moment the child is seen, all the pain seems to disappear.

Sometimes what makes us happy makes another person sad or even angry. We may even give up some activities that make us happy because the grief we receive afterwards, from others, outweighs the reward gained from that activity.

Because every individuals perspective on good and bad are not exactly the same we can only really rely on trusting our true soul. Those that are able to do this, live happy lives, those that don't are constantly fighting against life. Your soul is your own and everybody's soul is different. One set of rules can never achieve happiness for everyone; one size *DOES NOT* fit all.

Our soul is there to guide us towards happiness. It is on its own journey towards the Creator of the Universe. This Creator is pure and good and goes by many names. I leave it to you to decide which one to choose, but choose something that you understand has your best intentions at heart. Know that the name you choose stands for something that could never bring you harm, something that you can trust and only has love for you. This entity will never judge you, never punish you, instead it only adores you as if you are perfect in every way. It provides learning experiences that will eventually benefit our lives. It can see the long term evolvement, even if we can't.

We are perfect in every way and this *fact* is something that we need to begin to accept. It is something that we need to mentally digest. If we have done something bad, there will be a reason for it. There will be a background story and some good will have come out of it, unless we went against our own morals and were convinced by someone else to do this thing. If that is the case we should learn not to go against our own morals. We should not think of the bad things that others have done. Instead we should only concern ourselves with understanding the lessons we learned by doing any bad things ourselves. Knowing what you know now would have an influence on whether or not we would repeat doing that 'bad' thing? But put yourself back in the same situation with the same knowledge you had at that point in your life and you would still act and react the same way. Otherwise you would not be at this point in life now. That 'bad' thing that was done has had an impact on the way your life is lived right now. If it wasn't done, life right now would be different. Therefore regrets are a waste of precious thought energy. Instead, when it is learned to accept what has happened in the past and use those lessons to move forward, the future can begin to be shaped. When we keep looking back we will run into further issues in our future. Imagine turning your head so that you can't see in front of you and walk forwards. You will surely bump into something. If you faced forward you could see what's coming and prepare for it. When too much time is spent thinking about the past we become unprepared for what is happening to us now and in the future.

Looking backwards stops us from seeing what lies ahead.

It is never possible to be fully prepared. Life has a way of throwing situations and obstacles in our way, no matter how much preparation is made. Although history can teach us much of what has happened in the past, it does not hold all the answers for every individual situation in the future. In fact, not even with twenty first century technology can we find the answers for every single issue that rears its head. Let alone can we find the time to search through every source of information for all the answers? Our soul, however, can guide us through each and every situation. To learn how to receive this information is to learn to trust our own soul, our True-Self. This process of learning is only worthy of those who consistently practice it, meaning that by having a continuous awareness to receive the signs and advice provided. It requires a change of lifestyle. This can be easy, although it does require effort. That is what is meant by becoming a warrior. We contain the free will to make the choice to live the way of the Happiness Warrior.

I personally have made the decision to become a Happiness Warrior and would highly recommend it. This decision is a conscious one and I made it every second, initially. Then every second turns into every minute, then hour, until it quickly becomes automatic. An Olympic athlete is not a person who wakes up one morning and decides to take part in a sport that they have never tried before. Instead they train the majority of the day and night, both physically and mentally. The Happiness Warrior's lifestyle is just as intense, but it focuses on becoming aware of every moment and the clues offered, rather than living an auto-pilot life.

At the beginning of this journey, we need to remind ourselves of becoming more consciously aware. The more we practice the less we need reminding. Sooner than you may think, this process becomes natural, a new automatic. It is all about changing our perspective in order to find the silver lining. The positive result on health and happiness become apparent quickly. Others around you will notice a happier you and you will be able to share your secrets with them so that they too can become a Happiness Warrior.

Once we learn how to control ourselves we can enjoy what life brings. A sense of freedom, enlightenment, and happiness flows freely through our bodies and we begin to understand what is meant by truly living life.

Our Two Selves

As with any coin, there are two sides. In other words there are two opposite poles to everything. Below I have listed some examples under the categories of Physical and Spiritual.

Physical			Spiritual	
Hot	Cold		Faith	Pride
Dry	Wet		Hope	Anger
Front	Back		Charity	Envy
Day	Night		Temperance	Gluttony
Smooth	Rough		Justice	Lust
Above	Below		Strength	Sloth
Inside	Outside		Prudence	Greed

Figure 1. Physical Vs. Spiritual

Without each pole a comparison cannot be made. We cannot judge how good something is until it is possible to compare it with something bad. A person with only a front does not exist; they must also have a back. The two tables above are a clue to our own existence as we also have two sides, an environmental-Self and a True-Self. Our environmental-Self has been shaped and moulded by the physical world around us through our senses. Our sense of taste, touch, smell, sight and sound are continuously processing information from our environment. All this information shapes our ego. The other side of us is our True-Self; this is our spiritual Self, the Self driven by our instincts and gut feelings. All of our thoughts and judgements have physical and spiritual aspects to them. These thoughts and judgements then result in influencing our actions and responses. The more we react under the influence of our environmental-Self, the more of a challenge life will become. On the other hand, the more we react under the influence of our True-Self, the more life will become a pleasure. For example, if someone told you to wear a snow suit, scarf and gloves in a steaming hot sauna room, you should question their advice. Your instinctive Self would warn you with thoughts that something was not right. But instead you may decide to do what you were told. In this instance the advice from someone else has influenced your environmental-Self towards an action, you then did it, and therefore your reaction has completely ignored the warning from your True-Self. In this example the result of not listening to your True-Self could be fainting due to overheating and possibly even lead to other further health problems.

To become a Happiness Warrior the majority of actions taken should have their foundations in advice from our True-Self. Western philosophy, however, has always urged us towards focusing on the physical side even though humans are made up of both physical and spiritual substance. It is taught that science cannot prove the spiritual world, therefore, scientifically, it must not exist. This lack of knowledge on the spiritual side leaves the human race struggling with understanding the spiritual aspects of life on their own. Because there is little training in the spiritual aspects, when an inability to cope arises it often leads to depression, anxiety, and other mental concerns. Frequently, physical ailments have their roots in mental and emotional imbalances.

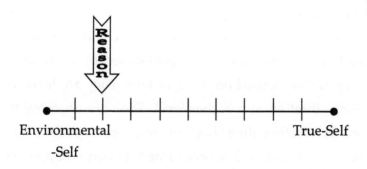

Figure 2. How our Reason is weighted

If we look at Figure 2, we can assume that most of our reasoning comes from our environmental-Self while we rarely use our instinctive abilities or guidance from our True-Self.

It is possible to live more instinctively. We already acknowledge the energy of the spiritual world through feeling it, as we have all experienced many of the spiritual aspects previously listed (Figure 1), such as anger or faith. Most of us have had an experience when we walk into a room and have felt uncomfortable, but could not explain why. We may also have experience of noticing that when a particular person walks into a room they are able to 'brighten the atmosphere' and lift the spirits of everyone in that room. This is possible because their energy frequency is so high that it spreads to others. Love is the highest spiritual energy in life and is unexplainable by scientists even though a number of them would have experienced love themselves. When someone is in love they can have a bad experience and not be concerned or overwhelmed by it, because they are so focused on being in love. They are holding their vibration at a higher level. They are choosing to feel love rather than dwell on negative situations. On the other hand, if that very same experience happened to someone who was angry, it might make them even angrier. This is because anger is a low vibrational frequency and a bad experience would further lower their vibration. But the person in love had such a high vibrational frequency that the bad experience may have lowered their vibration only a little, or they may not have even been affected by it.

A higher vibration allows instinctive guidance to flow

while a lower vibration cuts off access to instinctive guidance. The higher the vibration we hold, the more peaceful we become, the more instinctive we will act and the happier we will be. In this way we are guided by our True-Self, we feel less need to control, more present and creative. Our ability to successfully deal with day to day events increases and we open ourselves up to new experiences. Life becomes a pleasure. When we go against our gut feelings and take advice from our environmental-Self, we lower our vibration, encounter more problems, struggle with day to day events, and become more confused and unhappy.

"If we want peace, we must become peaceful inside."

∞ David Icke ∞

Is it possible to raise our energy frequency so that it shifts the balance towards being guided by our True-Self? YES! This is done through practice and gaining an understanding of who we are. Before we begin to understand who we are, I will explain how to shift the balance as well as shift the poles themselves.

In the example in Figure 3 the two poles, 0 miles and 1.0 miles, relate to the distance ran in 10 minutes. In the first month of training a runner manages 0.4 miles in 10 minutes. In the second month of training the runner manages 0.9 miles in 10 minutes. By the third month the runner has exceeded the previous 1.0 mile 'pole' and has shifted the poles upwards.

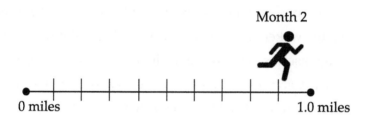

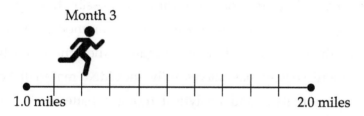

Figure 3. Shifting the Poles

Effectively we will always be on a scale with two poles at either end. We can make efforts to move up or down that scale; we can also go beyond that scale and create two new poles. This is all within our power. If you want more happiness in your life you will need to make the effort to achieve it. So how do we begin to shift our focus from the environmental-Self to our instinctive,

Higher-Self? Before this process can begin one needs to determine if the willingness is there to follow the process through, "do you have a spirit within you, so moving in its determination, that you can see things through so that you are authentically transformed" (Bachelor's Degree Curriculum, p. 2: 66)?

Everyone contains a spirit within to live a happier life, to awaken this one must acknowledge the two parts of themselves. Dr. Masters', in his *Ministers/Bachelor's Degree Curriculum*, writes that every person has two selves that exist within them. The first "...has been created by the conditioning of society, and usually has a limited appreciation of itself or its possibilities" (p. 1: 23). Our environmental-Self is more commonly known as the ego, its conditioning began at the time of birth, where society has successfully moulded materialistic, individualistic and analytical thought patterns, to the point where "...people hardly think for themselves..." instead, wastefully "...analyze every possible course of action..." (p. 1: 46). As I begin to explain the concepts of Western Civilization, it will be possible to start to understand its influence on our perspective, how it has the ability to manipulate our personality, or ego. The ego has succumbed to societies fear inducing and controlling techniques, leaving the belief that we are alone in this 'struggle of life' and have limited strength to accomplish anything that must be undertaken (p. 1: 57). We live in fear that "...poverty will result..." (p. 3: 1) if we rebel against the system, but at the same time we are told that we live in freedom (note the contradictive statement). What freedom do we actually have? We have the freedom of choice, but what choices are available? Is our freedom the right to choose what material goods we want to consume? Is this not slightly ironic? We live in a cycle of freedom to consume, which leads to debt, and then we are under its control. This cycle leaves our environmental-Self in a state of mental confusion, desperately searching for a bit of relief and happiness.

With all that we have been subject to within this society, we have become so distracted that our own personality has become dependent on fragmented, sporadic, and inaccurate information. According to the Office of the Surgeon General (US) in the article, *The Influence of Culture and Society on Mental Health*, "...20 percent of adults and children, in the United States have diagnosable mental disorders" (n.p.). Mental instability can cause "...schizophrenia, bipolar disorder, panic disorder, obsessive compulsive disorder, and other disorders..." (n.p). C.G. Jung confirms the mental impact of society when he said, "a certain kind of behaviour is forced on them [the people] by the world" (Jung, p. 123).

There is still hope. This hope appears as a spark which ignites from within and it is then realized that our survival does not depend on being tricked into destructive thinking patterns and compliantly behaving within the current dysfunctional social formalities. Without this spark, you continue to believe that society has not tricked you, that your personality purely comes from external events, people or circumstances and "you may go along with the majority of society, living a life of quiet frustration" (Bachelor's Degree Curriculum, p. 1: 47). At least while in the environmental-Self 'frame of mind' the perplexing question 'what is my purpose in life?' never needs to be tackled. But if for a moment, you can accept the possibility that the majority of your personality is controlled by your "...illusionary Self – which has been manufactured for us by the suggestions of others since childhood, when we first became conscious of our selves" (Bachelor's Degree Curriculum, p. 3: 13), then you must be open to discover what the remainder of your personality is composed of?

Our environmental-Self, or ego, has convinced us that there is nothing else we need in this world, that it is the only Self we contain, although it continues to leave us with an empty void in life, which no amount of material goods or pharmaceutical substances can permanently fill or treat. Some of us require the pressure of being backed into a corner, feeling as though we have hit 'rock bottom', in order to begin the search for our True-Self, but this book's purpose is to avoid that situation.

There is only one part of us that can answer the question of our purpose here and no matter how hard it is tried, the ego can never give a long-term fulfilling answer. The purpose of life cannot be answered in anybody else's words or teachings; otherwise it would have been done already. Scouring the internet for an answer will only lead in a spiritual direction. There is good reason for this, because the other part of our personality, our True-Self, contained within each and every one of us, knows our purpose on a spiritual level. This "...true selfhood will generate the power, confidence and Divine intuitive direction needed for the fruition of anything in life that one wishes to obtain or accomplish" (Bachelor's Degree Curriculum, p. 3: 28).

Generally, society relies on its ego, or environmental-Self, more so than its True-Self. For this reason we will begin by examining the environmental-Self. The more it is understood what we are not, but thought we were, the more we can understand what we really are.

This process of realization can be difficult for some. It is similar to a complex math equation. If you are unable to understand a full breakdown of every part of the equation, you just need to accept it for what it is. Many people struggle with math as a subject because they can't 'get their head around it'. This could be due to the need to understand every aspect of the equation and require seeing how it applies to something physical. Many times we are not shown how math equations are related to something physical and we are taught to accept it for what it is. Although we cannot see, touch, taste, smell, or hear love, we accept that it is still possible to experience. This acceptance is similar to accepting a math equation. The problem arises when we accept everything that is told to us as being the truth.

Each and every one of us contains a True-Self and the process of finding this is an individual journey. While reading about the environmental-Self all the information should be related to our own lives. At any moment, think of your own examples, from your own life, and apply the concepts being discussed. The more you can relate to these concepts, the easier it is to comprehend and understand.

♥ I WILL FIND MY TRUTH ♥

Our Environmental-Self

The Senses

Firstly, as our environmental-Self is a product of our environment, it is worth exploring the science and physics behind the human senses. This is the technical information which will show where external information comes from, how it is sensed, and how that information is electrically and chemically processed. This material has been heavily researched in order to bring a scientific understanding of how our own body works. Understanding this information will increase the ability to accept the concepts discussed further along.

In Harold Q. Fuller's book, *Physics: Including Human Applications*, he states that "your senses, your central nervous system, and your brain are the essential tools of science" (p. 8). All scientific experiments, their findings, and our learning from these findings have come about through the use of our senses. Without our senses we would have no scientific knowledge to pass on to future generations. Therefore science has to be treated as a perspective from the observer(s) doing an experiment. Fuller uses physics terms such as *interaction, variables, sensitivity,* and *discrimination,* which can be difficult to comprehend. In simpler terms, he describes the processing of information, within the human system, as independent parts which receive information and have the ability to manipulate that information into a form that allows the next part to understand it. For example, if we were never taught to speak the Chinese language, we would be unable to understand it when hearing it. The same applies to our instinctive-Self, if we have never acknowledged its existence; we would not know how to receive guidance from it.

Our bodies use electrical and chemical signals to communicate to other parts of itself. For example, when our body is lacking in energy we begin to feel hungry, we use our hands to collect and prepare food, chew it in our mouths, swallow it, and eventually our digestive organs transfer it into energy that our bodies can utilize. In this case alone, our brain has firstly received a signal that our body is lacking in energy, it then sends out chemical and electrical signals, in response, which put our body into motion in order to make food which requires the movement of muscles. The conscious action of consuming food is followed by digestion which transforms the energy from the food and uses it to refuel our body. This procedure requires our senses to work together, with our organs, while our brain continuously gives commands and receives input. Fuller explains that each part of our human system must obtain an input and process it so as to pass it onwards in a fashion it can be received by the next part. In the case of feeling a lack of energy through to digesting food, communication has occurred between many different parts within our body. If any part of our body system fails, the system fails as a whole. There is little requirement for us to be consciously aware of each individual step, in fact all the electrical signals and chemical changes taking place within our body happen at such a speed that our conscious awareness is unable to keep up. If we are not consciously aware of all the processing and manipulation of information within our own body-system, how can we be fully aware of the infinite effects our environment has on us?

Our senses are limited in how much information they can pick up. When our senses receive information from our environment, it is presented in varying intensities and our sensitivity will depend on our ability to process that information. Heightened sensitivity is due to our ability to accept greater amounts of detailed information as well as having greater means to process and understand it. If we are lacking in processing abilities, the information transferred becomes minimal and our sensitivity is lessened. This can be compared to lifting weights. If you have never lifted weights before, then your muscles will only be able to lift a small amount. If you train with weights often, they you will be able to pick up heavier amounts. Our sensitivity levels are determined in two ways, the amount of information our senses receive, as input, and our capability of modifying that input into a form the next part of our system can recognize. Fuller describes this input and output flow as a result of an action or influence between systems. If we hear a noise, our ears send information to our brain, the systems being our ears and our brain. Dependant on how our body sensors are equipped determines the information our sensors detect from interactions with our environment. If we had water in our ears, the vibrations picked up from a noise might be lessened and the brain receives a lesser signal. The sensors in our body can also distinguish between light intensity, color, sound intensity, sound frequency, taste, smell, temperature, pressure and tactile contact (Fuller, p. 8). Sensitivity is derived from our ability to respond to changes in the stimulus, or information received by the senses. If we hear the sound of an ambulance siren it is because it is louder than the other noises in our environment. The minimum amount of change detected is termed as the *threshold* and our ability to distinguish between two different stimuli is termed as *discrimination*. An experiment of our sensitivity *threshold* can be achieved by having numerous cups of water all of which are kept 1°C higher than the previous cup. If a finger was dipped into each cup, how many cups apart would it be until it was possible to feel the temperature difference? The minimum amount of cups apart, or 1°C temperature increase, would be the sensitivity *threshold*. If one of those cups had apple juice in them, which was noticed to be different to water, then we have *discriminated* between the liquids. Our bodies sensors can now be described in …terms of threshold, sensitivity and discrimination" (Fuller, p. 9). Breaking down sensors into these three categories is similar to breaking the description of a person down into the three categories of age, height, and weight. It is simply a means of further describing how our sensors work.

Figure 4 Mercury Thermometer

But how does our brain understand these categories? Fuller explains this using the example of a mercury thermometer to define *transduction* where the height of the mercury, in a tube, reacts to its environmental temperature. In this case, the external temperature causes a height change in the mercury which relates to numbers written next to them. Our brain reads the numbers and it is possible to accurately understand what the temperature is. As in Figure 4 it is possible to see that the temperature states around 37°C or 100°F. Here the mercury has expanded or contracted in the tube due to an increase or decrease in external temperature. A *transducer* is a sensor, or detector, that performs in this behaviour. Our senses work as transducer's converting the stimuli they receive into electrical signals which can then be transported and understood by the main control centre, our brain. The electrical signals travelling through our system hold information on the number of stimuli, the intensity of those stimuli, as well as discriminating between those stimuli. All of this information is then transformed into a readable format which the brain can understand.

Stimuli can come from direct or non-direct contact with its source. Either way, this interaction "...is an energy transfer between you and your environment"

(Fuller, p. 10). At this point I would like to stress the scientific confirmation that all the information our brain processes is fundamentally energy. Everything in this world is made up of energy. Everything we see, all the information we receive and even our own thoughts! This concept is not so difficult to understand. We have been taught to accept the existence of protons and neutrons and have an understanding of how tiny they are and accept that we are unable to see them with the naked eye. We have also been taught that radio waves and wireless systems work and yet we cannot see them with the naked eye. This is proof that energies are all around us even though we cannot see them. But why have we never been taught about our own gut instincts?

Let us now delve further by examining the senses individually. It is possible to recognize that "the sense of touch involves direct contact between you and our environment" (Fuller, p. 10). When we touch, or are touched by something, a force displaces the skin. Our brain then measures this displacement through our receptors. There are some places on our body where "the sensitivity of touch detectors… are able to detect the smallest contact force" (Fuller, p. 11).

Calipers (Figure 5) are a measuring instrument which have two points. The distance between those two points

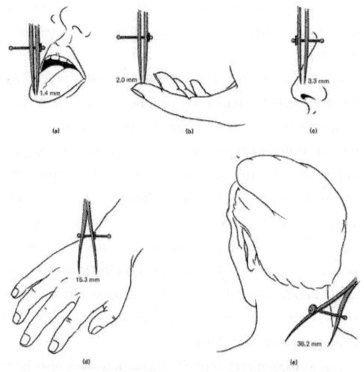

Figure 5. Fuller, Harold Q. – Calliper Measurements (11)

can be adjusted and measured. Touching the body with calipers has shown that the tongue can distinguish between the two points when only 1.4mm apart. The fingertips can distinguish a minimum distance of 2mm, while on the back of the neck the detectors are much further apart and are only sensitive in distinguishing the two points when they are a distance of 36.2mm (Fuller, p. 11). This is an indication of how our sensitivity to touch varies around our body due to differences in detector sensitivities as well as the distances between detectors.

Our sense of touch is not the only sense that requires "direct contact interactions" (Fuller, p. 11), taste and temperature also do. "Warmth and cold are sensed by two different types of receptors…, the forearm has approximately 10 times as many cold receptors as warm receptors per square millimeter" (Fuller, p. 12). Therefore we are more sensitive to feeling cold on our forearm than warmth. How our brain calculates the sensation of taste, with varying combinations of sweet, sour, bitter, and salty, is still unproven but evidence shows that "it is based on combined electrical and chemical processes" (Fuller, p. 12).

As well as direct contact interactions, we also have interactions-at-a-distance or non-direct interactions. For example, even though the sun is stated to be over 90 million miles away, we can still feel its heat and see its light, without the need to make direct contact with it. Fuller suggests that we imagine the distance between the two interacting systems, in this case, the sun and our body, as being connected by a field where the "second system is influenced by the changes in the first system through the change in its field" (Fuller, p. 13). Another example of a non-direct interaction is how a magnetic compass is influenced by the earth's magnetism. The earth produces a magnetic field which facilitates the alignment of the compass needle. Gravitational field's and electrical fields are further examples of non-direct influences interacting with our human system. These fields are sensed and have an influence over our physical body although they are not sensed through touch, taste, smell, sight or sound (Fuller, p. 13).

Our sense of sight can discriminate between distance, depth, and brightness, as well as perceiving color through a "wavelength of electromagnetic radiation" (Fuller, p. 13). The human eye is sensitive to an electromagnetic spectrum detecting "wavelengths between 3.9 x 10-7m (blue) and 7.0 x 10-7m (red) in length" (Fuller, p. 14), but not all wavelengths or colors are detectable within this 'visible' spectrum (see Figure 6). The human body also contains other electromagnetic wave receptors such as our skin receptors, which pick up infrared and ultraviolet wavelengths. Ultraviolet energy from the sun is chemically transformed by our skin receptors causing pigment changes such as suntans and sunburns (Fuller, p. 15). This is a further example of environmental influences on our bodies that our receptors sense, our body reacts to, although we are not consciously aware of them. Generally, education may introduce the concept of external influences on the human body, although the less you are aware of this information, the less you recognize it.

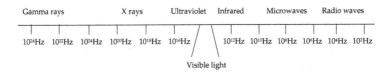

Figure 6. Electromagnetic Spectrum

Exploring sound, it is found to be "energy transmitted by pressure or density variations propagated through matter" (Fuller, p. 15). It is also possible to detect sound through our touch detectors due to pressure changes, although our ears are the most sensitive to these variations. As with sight, the human ear detects only a limited frequency range. Could it be possible that some people can detect frequencies outside of the 'normal' range? In the article "Super Powers for the Blind and Deaf," Mary Bates states "if one sense is lost, the areas of the brain normally devoted to handling that sensory information do not go unused-they get rewired and are put to work processing other senses" (Bates, p. n.p.). Her article explains that the rewiring in deaf individuals' affects how they perceive stimuli through their remaining senses, meaning their active senses can recognize things that hearing people don't. In this way the loss of one sense has heightened, or strengthened, the abilities and sensitivities of the remaining senses. This phenomenon is termed *cross-modal neuroplasticity* and research has shown that some areas of the brain are more plastic, or able to adapt, than others. Bates uses examples of blind individuals having 'enhanced auditory abilities' whereby people born deaf have greater abilities at processing peripheral vision as well as motion. She references research done on "13 congenitally deaf adults and 12 hearing adults" (Bates, p. n.p.), where the amount of blood flow within the primary auditory cortex section of the brain, was tested. Those subjects with hearing had less blood flow, than those without, when responding to stimuli through the sense of touch and sight. This increase in blood flow scientifically proves the heightened responses to touch and sight stimuli as being more active in deaf people.

A drawback to the way the brain compensates for missing sensory information is how it reacts when those senses return. For example, if someone gradually lost their sight at a young age and instantaneously regained it in later life, the immediate increase in sensory information requires the brain to rewire itself at a rapid rate. Marilyn Mendoza, in her article "After effects of the Near Death Experience" describes circumstances of immediate increases in sensory information occurring in Near Death Experiences (NDE's). She states "the after effects of an NDE...impact every aspect of the experiencer's functioning. It often takes years for individuals to incorporate these changes" (Mendoza, p. n.p.). Some documented NDE 'side effects' include a sense of awakening, increased openness towards others, higher self-esteem, the gaining of telepathic abilities, and precognition. These changes in perception and/or abilities can have a major impact on individuals' lives. In some cases, an NDE experience causes the individual to gain a sense of spiritual wholeness, although the increase in abilities can be a shock to the system as it can take the brain a while to adapt to this new found sensory information. These 'side effects' are also noted as being similar to the abilities of mystics, some of whom have not had "an 'instantaneous' life change... [rather the abilities have]... come incrementally, over a period of years" (Sinetar, p. 143).

James Redfield, in his book *The Celestine Prophecy: An Experimental Guide*, gives advice on how to become more attentive with our senses so that we can use them to attain peaceful, verging on meditational, states. When it comes to external clues we should be asking ourselves "what information is coming my way? What do I need to pay attention to here? ...By becoming more open to these 'little doorways' you increase your sense of adventure" (p. 12). He describes external clues as bits of information with the intention of guiding us, while also emphasizing that it is important to pay attention to our inner senses which give us very accurate feedback. For example, "if you are feeling a sense of heaviness or foreboding, you might need to slow down in order to delay a decision or to gain more information" (p. 12). Internal cues "such as tightening in the neck or stomach, clenching the jaws, loss of energy, shallow breathing, tapping fingers, crossed arms or legs, or irritation with sounds" (p. 13) can be signs that we are making decisions that are counterproductive or will result in future dissatisfaction. Listening to our internal guidance system is a skill that is better expressed by animals than humans. Redfield states that "in order to evolve... and the entire culture to thrive...people must open to the idea of allowing intuition to guide them back to a connection with the spiritual" (p. 27).

The Senses

Information comes at a constant stream, while our senses pick up on what is relevant to us "like a bold function key on the computer, intention selects out what we need to know" (Redfield, p. 69). When we begin to observe, without judgment or attachment, what our senses pick up we become "mindful of what is in front of us [and we begin] to connect with beauty and raise our consciousness to a higher level, thus enhancing our connection to spiritual energy" (Redfield, p. 79). In this way, when we consciously observe more, we are entering into light states of meditation, meaning we become more peaceful. Redfield suggests that when we eat an orange that we "notice its smell, texture, flavor, energy and the sounds of eating it" (p. 81) as this will fill us up with the energy of the fruit. Our environmental-Self, or ego, will sap us of energy with its need to win over others, but it is this time when we must fight back, "unhook ourselves from the need to control...We need not analyze other people or try to change them... [instead shift our] attention to tapping into the universal source of energy" (Redfield, p. 90). We can change our mood or vibration, by not ignoring the beauty of a tree as we walk past it or the fragrance of a flower on the breeze. Noticing these types of things will bring us into a better frame of mind, "make us feel truly alive"

(Redfield, p. 93), and bring more excitement into our lives. When we focus on our senses and become the *watcher*, we experience an "inner connection with divine energy" (Redfield, p. 128). Redfield suggests that "throughout the day, connect with the beauty in your environment as often as you can" (p. 232). Using our senses in this way will increase their sensitivity. The more we look, listen, taste, touch, and smell things that appeal to us, the more we appreciate things. This will attune our senses into focusing more on the things we love. The more our senses pick up on things we love, the better we become at noticing the things we love and the happier we become. In this way, our senses can help increase our personal vibration allowing for a happier and healthier existence.

The *Cambridge Dictionary* uses the term *ability* in its definition of the word *sense* as "an *ability* to understand, recognize, value, or react to something, especially [using] any of the five physical abilities to see, hear, smell, taste, and feel" (p. n.p.). Therefore when we sense something it must mean we have that particular ability to sense it. As our senses are available to us and allow us to notice things we appreciate, isn't it worth using them in this manner to improve our enjoyment of life?

The Senses

"You have a body
And exist
And are aware
Right at this very moment,
At this exact instant,
Because of a living Force
Within you"

(Barnes M. S., The Emerald Tablet 101, p. 52)

Western Programming

In the previous chapter, we have come to understand more about how the senses pick up information from our environment. In this chapter we will discuss how the information from Western culture has evolved its citizens into highly materialistic and individualistic human beings. Here we begin to understand the effect of Western programming on our environmental-Self. This part of us has unknowingly been conditioned by the system we inhabit to believe that happiness only comes as a result of success achieved through external efforts and the accumulation of materialistic goods. Having explored the senses, we know that happiness can be found in taking the time to watch a beautiful sunset, or smelling the scent of your favourite flower. But Western programming creeps in, trying to divert our focus towards success and money, convincing us that these two things are our only means to happiness. This programming urges us to become more interested in what is happening around us than what is happening within us. We have unknowingly been shifted from understanding what we felt inside to allowing what happens around us to dictate how we feel. The conditioning into this genus of life starts

43

at a very early age, yet when engrossed within this culture, humans are mostly unaware of the resultant negative effects on their own health and happiness. Let us begin to uncover some of the traps that have been laid, then later it can be shown where to direct our focus in order to achieve happiness, peace within oneself, and a sense of freedom even when contained within Western culture.

There is more to life than what we are aware of, in order to find our True-Selves we need to stop surrendering to the programming of Western Civilization. It is not acceptable to believe or live as "... slaves and a working force for a small clique of super-wealthy people..." (Penre, Beyond 2012, p. 3).

Geographically locating Western civilization is complicated as its boundaries are undefined. In his book *The End from the Beginning: The Origin of Western Civilization*, Clayton Willis describes the area as "... the British Empire, the commonwealth nations, [and] the United States of America..." (p. 245). Willis states that its beginnings emerged through the belief in a Creator of the universe, and the need to uncover an answer to the question *who was the Creator?* In an attempt to offer an explanation, religion developed through information which was orally passed down hundreds of generations until it was eventually documented in written form. The Bible defines Judaism and Christianity which are religions that "... are interwoven into almost every major event in the last 4,000 years... [which have]... not only affected the moral character of the people of Western Civilization but also were the basis of the legal and social foundations of its institutions, political character and governments" (p. 7).

With religious foundations, Western Civilization evolved followed through the surfacing of capitalism. With increasing sales, profits provided financial support to fund experiments and encouraging new thinking. These experiments became consequential to breakthroughs in manufacture and energy, which in turn, established the Industrial Revolution (Marr, p. 311).

In Andrew Marr's book, *A History of the World*, he discusses how the machine era "...that used the earth's stored energy (in coal and oil) [allowed production of] ...everything from cheap clothes to tinned food..." (p. 387). Niall Ferguson further confirms the advances in manufacture and energy in his book, *Civilization: The West and the Rest*, where he notes the ability to produce machines, which could manufacture textiles, providing a "...quantum leap in material standards of living for a rising share of humanity..." (p. 198). A definition of the words "material standards", means anything 'material' and outside of our minds, or anything of form. This focus on form pushed humanity to ignore the thoughts and feelings within their own minds. The result of thoughtlessness causes a blind leading the blind mentality where a few convincing leaders turned the majority of the population into followers. When we limit ourselves to only follow others, our creativity is lessened as is our confidence in breaking away from repetitive cycles and out of our own comfort zone.

As the general population began to lose confidence in itself, this left an opening for a minority of leaders to step forth. Profit driven leaders led countries rich in cotton to become rich in capital. The capital was invested in inventive skills which led to improve design and building machinery which enabled the mass production of clothing. According to Ferguson, the textile industry marked the heart of Westernization, and the beginning of the Consumer Society. The increase in production output meant more products to sell and an influx of profit. High profit, mass producing corporations required man power and the 'wage-slave' was born.

Economic growth inflated incomes as they rose from less than 0.2 per cent in 1760–1800 to 0.52 per cent in 1800–1830 up to 1.98 per cent in 1830–1870 (Ferguson, p. 199). This increase in wages meant that people still had funds left over after all the financial necessities of living had been taken care of. The excess of funds became another's opportunity for profit. Time and effort saving goods became the new means to make life more luxurious. Advertisements made appealing statements that mesmerised the public, almost hypnotising them into thinking that they were too good to pass up.

The desire for more of life's luxuries made people seriously consider their career choices, which then began to shift from low-paying agricultural employment to higher-paying jobs in manufacturing and services. It was the beginning of the greed driven consumer who became willing to sacrifice time with their family for more material goods.

In 1910 Western-invented and Western-owned railways, telegraphs, and steamship lines, reached across the world. The Industrial Revolution brought major mechanical advances in steamship horsepower causing ocean freight costs to fall over a third. This drop encouraged mass amounts of labourers to migrate

Figure 7. advertisingarchives.co.uk Image No. 30558229

from Europe to America, where "...up to 2.5 million migrants from South and East Asia travelled to the Americas" (Ferguson, p. 219). Along with people, products were also shipped worldwide increasing capital flow. With an amplified motive of efficiency and the availability of funding, further education increased in popularity and people realized how to work smarter rather than harder. Working hours in Europe steadily decreased from 1950 to 2000, as did religious beliefs and church attendance (Ferguson, p. 266). People shifted further away from inwardness and divinity, opting instead for external materialistic goods. In the 1960's consumer credit was introduced allowing those who didn't have the funding to purchase houses, have electricity, washing machines, and automobiles. Personal debt rapidly increased, trapping many individuals into employment that was mind numbing and lacking in personal satisfaction. Those who put themselves into debt held the weight of worrying about their debt which in turn stunted creative thinking. The only way to counter this wage slave, debt ridden lifestyle was to indulge in short lived satisfaction of consuming material goods. Millions in Europe and America were blinded by the fact that this came at the price of increasing debt and monotonous indoor jobs where workers retired, at the end of the day, to over populated, urban housing.

By 1973 half of homes had a color television (Ferguson, p. 238) and free time became increasingly spent being overloaded with information from television programs. Family time turned into the family sitting together in front of the television. Watching programs became a way to relax and switch off from the stresses of life. Very few considered that television could be detrimental. An article by Meghan

Neal discusses the effects that watching television has on the brain and points out that "mental rest is crucial... [yet watching TV] leaves the brain in a sort of limbo state of rest [where] neurons are still firing but the mind is not actually engaged [instead] it's taking in a boatload of information but not processing it" (Neal, 2016). In this hypnotic type state, so much information is thrown at us that we are unable to learn from it, utilize it, or to make "new connections that spark creative ideas" (Neal, 2016). Instead, television leaves us with the feeling of being depleted, lethargic, and with little to show for our time spent watching it. The information gained through watching television leaves us with a harassment of thoughts all of which are stopping us from achieving alpha wave cycles in the brain. Alpha brain waves make it possible to process information received throughout the day, digest it, and therefore produce a relaxed frame of mind.

The negative effects of material goods were not limited to information overload from television programs and debt; mass production began to take its toll on the earth with natural resources beginning to deplete causing deforestation, the extinction of species; overfishing and pollution (Marr, p. 387).

This didn't deter the general public as, despite any personal debt, their greed for material items outweighed their concern of the detrimental effects the Industrial Revolution had on the environment. Advertising was far more influential than any instinctive need to care for the earth. Acquiring more material goods seemed to be the only way to achieve happiness, albeit only temporarily. Clever advertising on the television, in newspapers, and magazines, taught us how much happiness costs and where to 'purchase' it. Consuming material goods became part of people's personality. It began to govern their well being, where happiness was gained through the purchasing and ownership of luxurious goods while sadness and fear were experienced due to the debt caused by the financial means to afford them. A never-ending cycle. Everyone wanted the luxuries that their neighbours had; it became a competition to have the best 'things'. All these 'things' started accumulating to the point where rented storage became available to house any excess.

Our environmental-Self has been manufactured through information received from numerous external sources. In early education we are taught several subjects in school, much of that information we may not even utilize in our career, and rarely does it contain basic survival skills, yet we believed it to be the truth and never questioned it. Are we only taught subjects, deemed necessary, at school because they are socially and politically acceptable points of view? Why are there no subjects on how to improve our instinctive abilities, to question anything that we cannot prove for ourselves? Without conducting an experiment on any theory for ourselves, we are putting our trust into someone else's perspective. When we put trust in something outside of us we allow it to take control. How many subjects or pieces of information have we put our trust in? How many concepts or people have we allowed to control us? When will we stop blindly following the controlling factors in our external life and begin to question and investigate our natural, instinctive-Self; the part inside us that generates happiness and success?

In his lecture, *Life is NOT a Journey*, Alan Watts states that Westerners only choose to focus on the end point, or goal, rather than the journey itself. Watts states that this focal point has come from societal conditioning starting within the education system. He says that initially most of us are excited to begin school. We watch our older siblings or friends attending school and hear stories about playing games, creating art, and learning how to read. School also teaches us how to behave socially and that our success in the first year is measured through graduating into the second year. All of our educational years are then spent trying to achieve the goal of progressing onto the subsequent years which continues throughout high school, college, graduate school, and so forth, until we are thrown into the real world where we have been programmed to then find a lucrative career. Once employed, we find ourselves ever more chasing success through achieving quota's, and with each accomplished, another quota is supplied. We are endlessly chasing the next thing until we briefly stop for a moment in our mid-forties and believe we've achieved our goals. After congratulating ourselves, in a momentary pause, we realize we need to prepare for retirement, putting off enriching life experiences in favour of saving money for times when our bodies are old and incapable of enjoying those experiences (Watts, 2017).

Throughout our lifetime, from the start of our formal education, we are taught to focus on the future. We understand that the past has an impact and we often dwell on the so-called wrong decisions we have made. Happiness is only achievable in the present moment, yet we tend to spend very little time in the present. It is easy to remember a time in life where we were happy, but that has a negative impact on us because we come to realise that *now* we are not happy, which lowers our vibration and leads to depression. If we focus on the future, the vast unknowingness of potential outcomes and hurdles causes us to become anxious. Western Civilization has torn us away from being content and happy in our own skin, in our own existence, but the foundation of its control has always been through the creation of fear.

Fear – A Controlling Tactic

In Alexander's paper, *The Civilization of Fear*, he talks about fear being the major controlling factor in our lives and how authority has gained the ability to keep the general public in fear. "A state motivates a person to behave in a certain way by means of fear – the fear of punishment" (p. 2). Alexander describes a 'state' as one of two types of authority, firstly as economic levers such as the police and the military, of which their goal is to protect peoples' lives and their property from both external threats. The second type of authority is described as 'money-power' or debt.

We have already discussed how a consumer society generates debt which results in the wage-slave. The wage-slave lives in fear of a lack of funds which brings worries that they will not be able to provide for their dependants. This fear inducing tactic provides a civilization within which "all we risk being left with are a vacuous consumer society and a culture of relativism – a culture that says any theory or opinion, no matter how outlandish, is just as good as whatever it was we used to believe in" (Ferguson, p. 288). In other words, when the public has an instilled sense of fear, they are more likely to believe any untruths when provided.

Returning to the subject of televisions, why are they full of programs? Television programs contain theories and opinions that humans, as a race, have become so dependent on that all the information provided is considered as the truth. It is as though we are actually *being* programmed by them. Wes Penre, in his book *Introductory Level of Learning*, talks of being "bombarded with information and propaganda wherever we are. We are constantly fed with opinions, bad news and lies...Our survival is threatened constantly, at least that's how it seems, and this is primarily occupying our thinking these days...Much of this fear and terror is spread through the Media" (Penre, p. 2).

History shows us many examples of how easy it is for the Media to spread fear through convincing the people of untruths. One of the most historically prominent events was the broadcast, on October 30th 1938, which described an alien invasion. Upon hearing, either first or second hand, of this invasion, thousands of Americans became panic-stricken (Cantril, p. vii). "In a New York studio of the Columbia Broadcasting System", Orson Welles and a small group of actors read an adapted version of the novel *War of the Worlds* by H.G. Wells. The following day the newspapers printed about the "tidal wave of terror that swept the nation". People believed that "monsters armed with death rays were destroying all armed resistance sent against them; that there was simply no escape from disaster; that the end of the world was near" (Cantril, p. 3). In current times it seems difficult to fall for such obvious examples of unjustified media instigated panic, but this is still the case. The media continue to spread panic, report falsities, construct events using actors, and spread propaganda. Even in the year 2020, the media have convinced the world that the fate of humanity is doomed. The few who have closer ties with their spiritual side realise that the media is unjustly spreading fear and instigating panic. The detrimental effect of these fears are felt by many both mentally and physically.

On a physical level, there are many psychological tricks used to instil fear. The police forces are here to protect the community and they do that through controlling criminal activity. Their uniform is dark and usually equipped with numerous items to protect themselves and others. This equipment is strapped onto them giving the impression that they are bigger than they really are. On some occasions they may wear hats or protective headgear, which also gives the impression that they are in control and therefore able to control a situation.

Authority, within a working environment, is usually achieved through experience and controlling abilities. Experience gives strength to controlling abilities, although sometimes the controlling abilities are so strong in some individuals that experience isn't even required. A respected boss will be able to be stern and fair, as well as giving clear instructions. A boss who does not have control will not get the best out of their workforce. All types of control can be analyzed in terms of a see-saw effect of energy. In order for someone to have control, another must willingly give up their control. In an energetic manner, the controller gains energy from the person willing to give up their control and energy. In order for the government to have control, its people must give up their control. In order for the teacher to instil learning in class, the students must accept the lessons. This transfer of energy is everywhere, in every situation.

Our True-Self recognises the transfer of energy and it gives us clues when and where it happens. If someone got reprimanded by their manager, they would feel upset, become tired, as though they were lacking in energy. This is actually the case as energy has been transferred from the employee to the manager. From that point on the employee may live in fear of being reprimanded again, or fear losing their job. In order to avoid being further reprimanded, similar mistakes are avoided and feared. This type of fear has come through a particular negative experience, but what about fear that has no previous experience? Vivekananda tells a story of a baby chicken fresh out of its egg, "…where an eagle comes, and the chicken flies in fear to its mother" (Vivekananda, p. 127). He asks what makes the chicken fear death from an eagle? How does the chicken even know fear or that its life is at risk, and how does it know that the eagle is an enemy? There has been no opportunity for teaching from its mother as the chicken has only just emerged into this world, so it must be instinct.

Intuitive thoughts, generated through our instincts, come to us from our True-Self or Higher-Self, a Self that is free of "...misery which comes from fear..." often generated by unsatisfied desire (Vivekananda, p. 183). This unsatisfied desire is driven by the false beliefs that we have lost control and that the consumption of material goods will bring longevity of happiness. Desire is describing a want or need that is not available now and only available in the future. Happiness can only be experienced in the *now* moment. The more we are present in the *now* moment the less we desire and the happier we become. Happiness gained through the purchasing of 'objects' are short lived moments which are soon followed by the desire for more, again leaving an unsatisfied hole within us. Vivekananda states that the only method to acquire eternal bliss is to achieve the knowledge of concentration on one's own mind. Our focus should be turned inwards on the constant pursuit of perfecting ourselves. It is more important to fix ourselves, our perception of things, than it is to fix the majority of external things. If we are not living in the belief that we are our best Self, how can we improve anything else?

In order to find ourselves "we have to stop being afraid, free our mind, [and] really start to think deep" (Alexander, p. 2). How can it be that Buda's and mystics, who spend a large amount of time meditating, never belittle others? Is it because they have found a deep sense of peace within themselves and therefore have no need to steal energy from others? Have you ever noticed that those who ridicule others have deep unresolved issues and tend to act artificially rather than truthfully? Gossiping is a sure sign of insecurity. Those who gossip are only doing so to gain the acceptance of others. This act causes separations and it is likely to backfire. If one talks badly to another person they are less likely to receive help from that person. Why would one ever want to deny themselves help from another? This is not how the Creator works, so where did this behaviour come from? These are the sorts of thoughts and questions that we should be asking ourselves, all the time. The more we understand how we act and react the more we can examine the origins of our actions and reactions.

Examining our own emotions is an extremely powerful practice. Just by acknowledging them we are moving our conscious attention into the *now* moment, the present. When our senses pick something up, a stimulus, and an emotion is sparked within us, our brain stores the stimuli plus emotion as a combination. This emotional information effectively attaches itself to the stimuli originally received. Our brain stores away this combination waiting until the next time we encounter the same stimuli. When the same stimuli returns our memory associates the same emotion from our past experience bringing it into the present moment. This combination is stored in deeper levels of the mind than our conscious awareness, in the sub-conscious mind. The sub-conscious mind is ready and waiting to re-attach the specific emotion to the stimuli recorded with it previously. To expand on emotion and stimuli combinations we also "associate different emotional words with different sensory qualities" (Rago, 2014), meaning that "our emotions and sensory cortices can impact one another in both directions" (Rago, 2014). This attraction of an emotion to sensory input, or words, is *the* key to discovering how contaminated our senses are. The contamination occurs in the emotion related to the sense, where the emotion needs to be firstly observed and then examined in order to determine its origin. The emotions origin will either be from our True-Self, or it will be from an external source. If it comes from an external source it can be classed as coming from our ego or environmental-Self.

Neuroimaging has shown that our sensory cortices are activated at higher rates, in response to emotions. Fear and love are the two highest activators. When touched by someone we love, the sensitivity of our skins touch detectors increase, as well as attracting loving emotions to the signals sent to the brain. If our sensitivity is heightened when we experience higher vibrational emotions such as love, they then must be reduced when experiencing lower vibrational emotions such as hate or fear.

In 2010, Sacco and Sacchetti conducted an experiment on rats showing that there is a secondary sensory cortex that stores emotional memory, which we associate with the same or similar sensory input (Rago, 2014). "Our emotions and senses are very tightly intertwined. What we hear, see, taste, smell and touch can provide us with information on how to feel" (Rago, 2014). This feeling is derived from emotions such as like, dislike, love, hate or fear.

Have you ever sat down and watched a movie and become consciously aware of its effects on your emotions? Have you ever cried at a movie? Are you aware of all the emotion and sensory combinations that are forced upon us through our environment? It has already been discussed that watching television puts our brain into a limbo state where it us unable to consciously process the vast amount of information that is thrown at us. How much of this information is bypassing our conscious awareness and headed straight to our sub-conscious mind creating emotion plus stimulus combination? These combinations were not even experienced by us, they were only viewed in movies. But can our mind comprehend reality and non-reality when the advances in computer simulation can make movie stunts look so real? What is happening within the sub-conscious mind when playing computer games with realistic graphics? Has there been any increase in violence since the introduction of war-type computer games? Imagine if this type of programming was in the wrong hands, it could have the power to convince all the individuals in the world to do many things they would not morally even consider doing. If we do not study our emotional responses to things, we respond and react in an auto-pilot manner and that manner may have been programmed into us. The more we react unconsciously the less control we have of ourselves and our situations. The opposite of auto-pilot is becoming consciously aware. Becoming consciously aware within the *now* moment of our emotions allows us to choose our reaction and action. This free will choice becomes fully under our control. Decisions made in this frame of mind will bring happiness and success.

Are our feelings influenced socially? As adults we tend to respond in ways that are socially acceptable, while as children we respond more so from our True-Self. Is this because, over time, our ego has become influenced through a fear of being socially unacceptable? Have we built up a memory bank of emotional responses that restrict us and our own creativity? Whatever we touch, see, smell, hear, and taste is all external to us, a part of our environment or physical reality. We do, however, posses the ability to choose our emotional response to any environmental stimuli.

Fear is a negative, lower vibrational, emotion and in order to counteract this, the body depletes its own positive energy. This balancing procedure leaves our bodies lacking in energy. We become tired and irritable. Decision making becomes more difficult and we resort to following the advice of others rather than searching within ourselves for positive solutions. When we live in fear, we tend to live in a world that seems beyond our control. This is because we have given over our control. It is a manufactured cycle that has been put in place to keep us in our place, leaving only a few with power.

Failures of Science and Technology

We have seen that Western Civilization has emerged from the scientific revolution to the industrial revolution bringing us into the technology age. The advances in technology are supposed to make our lives easier, but instead leave us feeling exhausted, unfulfilled and overloaded with information to the point where we have no time to focus on our inner being.

The distractions technology provides have turned into addictions. It has become much easier to look at our phones for irrelevant information than to look at ourselves and improve our own lives. Having the latest products, due to influential advertising of 'new and improved' versions, encourages purchasing better versions of the products we already have! To keep up with fashionable technology incurs great financial pressures, yet many believe this worthwhile faced with the risk of becoming left behind or social outcasts. Advertising is blatant programming of one's environmental-Self, guiding us towards debt in a never ending cycle. As humans become increasingly dependent on readily available media, they become the unwilling subjects to propaganda and advertising's sub-conscious manipulation of the decisions we make. Filled with miracle answers to all of our individual issues, advertising convinces us to spend our hard earned money, on things we don't necessarily need. The products we purchase promise to dramatically change our life for the better. What happens when these products don't turn out to improve our lives? Luckily, by the time this has been realised there is a new and improved version that promises to do the job properly. Temporary happiness gained, through these purchases, diminishes quickly and becomes short lived. Technology leaves us with voids in life, an emptiness inside, due to the fact that external 'things' or 'places' will never sustain our inner happiness. How have we allowed this programming to take over and convince us of what we need in life, convince us that all answers come externally?

Leyland Barrows quotes Andrew Targowski's book *Western Civilization in the 21st Century*, when he states that "...excessive profit-driven and information technology-assisted global business which works for global corporations but not for citizens of developed nations whose jobs are being exported to countries with low costs of labor" (Barrows, p. 118 qtd.). This statement explains that modern corporations are more concerned with increasing their profit margins and less with the welfare of the people. Targowski finds a growing population becoming individualized through the rapid increase in technology and computerization causing the population's social skills to diminish through their repetitive use of social media.

Social media is not even *social*; in fact it has a detrimental effect on communication skills such as reading and writing. In the need to respond quickly, words become abbreviated or spelled incorrectly. It is as if texting and messaging has formed its own language. How has it come to be that happiness is determined by the number of virtual 'likes' or 'subscribers' and not by how we feel inside? I use the term 'virtual' because it is not even guaranteed that the 'liker's' or 'subscribers' are known to you, or even real people. If someone disagrees with a comment made on social media, their response can be aggressive or even hurtful. One negative comment can circle the thoughts of the reader who takes it personally, possibly even having a major impact on their lives. Bullying on social media is responsible for numerous suicides. The negative consequences of technology can be seen in many restaurants where couples or families spend valuable time together, a chance to catch up with everybody's lives, but instead of sharing stories, everyone is on their own phone, doing their own thing, isolating themselves. This isolation has severed the ability to obtain support from physical people, resulting in the need to deal with life's pressures on one's own. This isolation, compounded with the pressures that society puts on us, is a destructive cycle that comes at the expense of our mental and physical health.

We are socially separating ourselves with the ever increasing technology at our fingertips, feeding an egoic 'them and I' mentality. Social media is removing our ability to say 'hello' to the people we walk past, instead it is putting us at risk of walking straight into them as our eyes are glued to the screen on our phones. Jung says "…mankind, because of its scientific and technological development, has in increasing measure, delivered itself over to the danger of possession" (Jung, p. 253). The possession, referred to in this statement, is caused by the influx of information received about what products to buy, how to look, behave, and act. Western civilization has used the immense power of technology to convince the human race to, not only doubt our ability to function in the world, but has also stripped our ability to believe that we have a choice. We must begin to ask ourselves the questions 'is this information relevant to me?' and 'why am I surrendering my wellbeing to something or someone who does not know me, let alone know what is best for me?'

In his book *The Four Paths of Yoga*, Swami Vivekanada says "...the Western(er)... says, build a good house, let us have good clothes and food, intellectual culture, and so on, for this is the whole of life; and in that he is immensely practical. But the Hindu says, true knowledge of the world means knowledge of the soul, metaphysics; and he wants to enjoy that life" (p. 101). The difference here is that the Westerner has been convinced that items of form, those made of matter, which can be seen or touched, have material substance, and are external from the mind, these are the things which we are taught, bring joy to life and substance to our personality. Whereas the Hindu find happiness by focusing on non-form aspects which cannot be associated with the senses, energies which are internal, knowledge of the Soul, and one's presence within the Universe. Vivekanada follows on to say that "from our childhood upwards we have been taught only to pay attention to things external, but never to things internal; hence most of us have nearly lost the faculty of observing the internal mechanism" (p. 183). This internal mechanism Vivekanada refers to is awareness itself and our connection to our own internal, or Higher-Self.

There is no quick-fix. Imagine if our advanced technology was able to design a pill which could allow our brain to expand upon our currently limited perception, our senses could be instantly heightened, and we could become aware of so much more than we currently are. *Limitless* is a film where the main character, Eddie Morra, is struggling with writers' block and gains access to a fictional pill, NZT48, which increases his abilities. This new, unreleased, FDA approved drug, "identifies the receptors in the brain that activate specific circuits" (n.p.).The drug, NZT48, enables 100% access to the brain, which is an increase from our current usage of 20%. In the movie,

Eddie returns to his apartment block and swallows the pill while walking up the stairs to his apartment. Greeted by his angry neighbour, he can feel his senses starting to activate. Everything he see's becomes illuminated with vibrant colors as he gains the ability to see beyond the visible spectrum. His hearing is instantly improved and he can readily access unconscious memories of relevant information. This proves beneficial as he uses the available information, from these forgotten memories, to calm his neighbour down then outwits her with his remembered knowledge and new perception. His confidence soars and he is filled with the energy to tidy himself and his apartment up. He consciously notes a new found clarity of mind where he "knew what to do and how to do it" (n.p.). With his mind clear and his apartment tidy, he sits down at his laptop and starts writing. The next morning he feels back to normal as the abilities the drug gave him had disappeared, leaving him only with his laptop upon which he notices numerous pages written. Now addicted to the new found power and abilities, Eddie takes some pills and finishes his book in four days. He finds his brain is so adaptive that he can learn to play the piano in minutes and pick up foreign languages just by hearing a few words spoken around him. His popularity among others escalates rapidly and he discovers a new attitude filled with confidence, vanquished of any previous fear or shyness.

In the movie *Limitless*, Eddie found he had the ability to access previous, relevant, information. This information was originally received months, years, or even decades earlier and therefore not in his conscious awareness. Instead this information was accessed through his subconscious where the fictional drug had enhanced his ability to do so. Taking this fictional drug resulted in no adverse effects from rapid brain rewiring caused by heightened abilities and sensitivities. When we have a flash of a memory, it is not because we were consciously thinking about it, more so it will be our subconscious mind feeding it into our conscious thoughts. These flashes occur at a rate that we can process in order to not over work the functionality of our brain. Instead of a quick fix we must slowly integrate our awareness and this process can take many years. Confidence, believing that you are capable, and practice will increase skill levels to achieve heightened sensitivities.

Why does science seem so unknowledgeable outside the realms of the main five senses even though there are many physical sensors within the human body of which we are consciously unaware of? Could it be that scientists have contaminated their own senses, due to methodical approaches and limited equipment, causing them to become unable to prove the process of increasing sensitivity? Is this why there are unfounded 'scientific' explanations in the cases of sudden increases in abilities, such as the after effect of NDE's (Near Death Experiences)?

In an article by Fiona MacDonald, she describes how Rueben Nsemoh was a native English speaker who knew some basic Spanish. After suffering a concussion during a soccer game, he slipped into a coma where upon awakening; he fluently spoke Spanish and struggled with the English language. In this case "Doctor's are struggling to explain exactly what happened [to Rueben]" (p. n.p.). It seems that those who limit themselves to previously documented 'so-called' facts are the ones who struggle to define and prove this type of phenomenon. Maybe this and similar cases have no rational explanation that can be proven through current scientific experiments. Only those who focus on the spiritual aspects of existence can actually relate and explain these experiences. There will be no evolution for the human species if we limit ourselves to proven theories. Instead we must shift towards more imaginative, creative, and outside the box thinking such as the great minds of Albert Einstein and Nicola Tesla.

The Abilities of Animals

There are many creatures on earth that seem to have natural abilities and sensitivities beyond those of humans. "Animals have abilities that we have lost. One part of ourselves has forgotten this; another part has known it all along" (Sheldrake, p. ix). In Rupert Sheldrake's book, *Dogs That Know When Their Owners Are Coming Home and Other Unexplained Powers of Animals*, he proves through various experiments, the astonishing abilities of animals. Sheldrake studied sciences at Cambridge University and gained a Ph.D in biochemistry which led him into animal testing. His love for animals forced him to put a stop to conducting fatal tests and instead he began to focus his research on what pets could teach us. He gathered over 500 reports about dogs being able to sense when their owners were coming home. Covering every possibility, he proved that this ability was not limited to the familiar sound of the family car, smells of their owner's sent or due to regular arrival times. In fact, owners could use the train, walk, arrive in a taxi, get home at varying times, and still the dog would "react when the person sets off to come home or is preparing to do so" (p. 41). One case study involves a dog becoming restless at 4:45pm and moving to sit at the window. Moments later it returned to its basket and at 5:15 pm it became excited and moved back to the window, where it stayed until its owner arrived. The dog sitter was amazed to hear that the owner had decided to leave for home at 4:45, then changed their mind, and eventually decided to leave at 5:15 (p. 47). Sheldrake's explanation of this phenomenon is that the dogs' sense of knowing comes telepathically, or in his words, through a morphic field which is formed by a bond that links dog and owner. He describes this morphic field as an elastic band which can stretch and contract, connecting a dog and its owner. At the moment the owner decides to leave for home, a message travels along the band as vibrations which alert the dog. Some cases show the dog can even be asleep and the vibrations are strong enough to awaken the dog when they are received.

The loving bond between animals and their owners creates a telepathic link which animals are more sensitive to than their owners. Monks, Mystics, and Shamans are human beings with heightened sensitivities closer to those of animals, while the Native American Indians use this awareness to communicate with the animals themselves. Are these enhanced abilities the result of intuitively based thinking rather than rationally based? These individuals question the difference between the two sides of their thinking throughout their lives. They are aware of their rational side or environmental-Self, although they are more influenced by the purity of animals, Nature, the World, and all other energies that guide them to their, pure, True-Self.

Sheldrake states that humans can "pick up other people's feelings though body language and other sensory information" (p. 93), where as animals are also sensitive in this way. When a member of a herd of flock selflessly alerts other members of the group to danger, it risks its own survival by catching the attention of a predator. This selfless act shows that some species, with a social bond between them, can express empathy. Over two hundred cases show that animals' stay "close to people who are sick or sorrowful, as if to comfort them" (p. 94). Many of those cases even proved that "sometimes dogs also seem to know what part of the person's body is painful, and comfort them where it is needed" (p. 98). It can be said that "humans are generally less sensitive to their animals than animals are to their people" (p. 113). Sheldrake provides a study of fifty-five reports of animals reacting to the distant death of their owners but only seven owners had reported knowing that their pet had passed away.

Sheldrake's studies show that wild animals, in social groups, have bonds so strong that they are unable to lead isolated lives. Their "complex social organization occurs even among the lowest animals, such as corals and sponges" (p. 155). The morphic fields within these groups provide the ability to coordinate the creation of nests and other structures. Sensory communication through scent trails, touch and vision are inadequate to "explain how termites, could build such prodigious structures, with nests up to 10 feet high, filled with galleries and chambers and even equipped with ventilation shafts" (p. 157). Eugene Marais observed the repair of large holes created in the mounds of an Eutermes species. The workers, who are blind and never came into contact with each other, repaired holes on different sides of the mound joining them correctly together. Marais attributed the overall organization to a 'group soul' (Sheldrake, p. 158 qtd.).

When under attack, schools of fish turn sharply outward, leaving a hole around their predator. They reverse their direction and reassemble, never colliding.

In laboratory tests, fish have even been temporarily blinded and still school normally, proving they do not rely on their sight to accomplish this feat (Sheldrake, p. 159). Sheldrake puts forward the theory that animals contain telepathic abilities independent to the known senses. The "feelings communicated telepathically include fear, alarm, excitement, calls for help, calls to go to a particular place, anticipation of arrivals or departures, and distress and dying" (p. 167). If these abilities, "beyond the range of sensory communication" (Sheldrake, p. 168), are active and utilized by animals, what dormant abilities do human beings contain?

Sheldrake discusses further animal abilities, such as finding their own way home. Pets have been recorded as falling asleep in cars, escaping and making their way home miles further than familiar smells could guide them. He is most impressed by the abilities of birds; two Laysian albatrosses "were taken from Midway Island…and released from Washington State, 3,200 miles away, one returned in ten days, the other in twelve. A third came back from the Philippines, more than 4,000 miles away, in just over a month…After nearly a century of dedicated but frustrating research; no one knows how they do it. All attempts to explain their navigational ability in terms of known senses and physical forces, have proved unsuccessful" (p. 188). The human sense of direction seems to be the strongest in traditional peoples, including "Australian Aborigines, the Bushmen of the Kalahari, and the navigators of Polynesia" (Sheldrake, p. 191). These people lived a much more organic life and had to rely on their senses and instincts. Modern man, with numerous artificial navigation aids such as global positioning systems (GPS), has reduced the requirement for the use of these instinctive abilities (Sheldrake, p. 192).

Many animals have shown to have abilities to forewarn humans through their unusual activities of an impending epileptic fit, seizure, or even earthquakes. Sheldrake reports a case where a woman's dog started sniffing around a lesion on her leg and if she wore shorts the dog would try to bite the legion off. After several months of her dog's strange behaviour, she went to the doctors to find the legion was cancerous and had it removed (Sheldrake, p. 241).

On the morning of February 4th 1975, a decision was made to evacuate Haicheng, due to animals' panicking and acting very strangely. The very same evening, at 7:36, an earthquake that reached 7.3 on the Richter scale hit and could have killed tens of thousands of people (Sheldrake, p. 249). Theories that animals may be attuned to subtle sounds, vibrations, gasses released by the earth, or electrical differences are still unable to explain these types of animal premonitions (Sheldrake, p. 255).

The human body seems to show similar abilities of prediction, although humans are mostly unaware of them. In an experiment, at the University of Nevada, humans' blood pressure, skin resistance and blood volume were monitored through their fingertips. They were shown positive, relaxing, images of landscapes and cheerful people, with a few emotionally negative images randomly thrown in. "The remarkable feature of the results is that the arousal began [about 4 seconds] *before* the emotional[ly negative] images appeared on the screen, even though nobody could have known by any normal means which picture was coming next" (Sheldrake, p. 265). Sheldrake wonders if brain evolution, through "civilization, literacy, mechanistic attitudes, and dependence on technology" (p. 269), have caused our sensitivity to diminish as compared to the sensitivity of animals.

When we evaluate our lives against the lives of animals, we can see how different they are. Humans and animals are both subject to social and survival matters although these matters take on very different forms. Humans have a tendency to think more in terms of the future and the past, while animals are very much present in the now. Are humans missing out on important evolutionary information, received through the senses, by distracting themselves through conjuring up numerous outcomes and potential solutions to irrelevant problems? In this way are we sacrificing time which could be better spent digesting, or processing, the input received through the senses? Most animals, after a confrontation, have the ability to 'shake it off' and walk away from the confrontation. Humans instead seem to hold onto or suppress confrontations without fully processing them. If we don't use these processing abilities we *will* lose them.

The human body contains numerous ways of sensing our environment. We can detect things that come into contact with us through our touch detectors; we can also detect things that don't come into contact, such as the warmth of a flame. We are aware of some receptor activity but unaware of others, such as when our skin receptors pick up ultraviolet energy. What is notable is the manipulation of information received by our sense detectors as it travels towards our brain, picking up further information from deeper levels within our mind. "The lower animals have Consciousness but ...

they cannot travel with their minds, or create as you and I can…no other living creature has your level of consciousness" (The Hermetica 101, p. 39). Humans have access to deeper levels of consciousness than animals, although our ego is more susceptible to external influences which limit our abilities to reach them.

Our True-Self

"We say that the two parts of us are the soul and the body, our mind and matter" (Castaneda, p. 126). Our environmental-Self, in its madness, attempts to make perfect sense of everything around us. While our minds are busy doing this we are restricting our instinctive abilities and limiting access to deeper levels within our own mind. Light meditational states are achieved when we become consciously aware of the information transmitted to our brain, originating from our senses. When we practice any examination of what is happening to us emotionally we gain the ability to reach the deeper levels of our mind. Here we are working on a conscious level, in the *now* moment, which brings clarity and peace.

Our True-Self "is the spark of life that causes you to have existence" (Masters P. L., p. 1: 23), "...a Higher Mind [which] exists within that can answer all things" (Masters P. L., p. 1: 46). When we have "...an awareness of the illusions that can take over one's life as a result of being guided by personal egotism" (Masters P. L., p. 1: 47), it is possible to begin to study the phenomenon of our instinctive nature. We have started with how our senses and environment have shaped us; this needed to be the first step. Without this comparison it is impossible to see what isn't our True-Self and what is.

I call the opposite of our environmental-Self our True-Self as it is the Self which will guide us towards evolution. It is the Self that is instinctive, connected to Divine guidance. Our True-Self is connected to our Soul; it takes guidance from higher vibrational levels. The higher the vibration, the purer, lighter, and more Divine it is. The lower the vibration, the darker, heavier, and more disruptive it is. Being sensitive to these vibrations allows us to decipher the truth through signs and clues. These clues are everywhere but unless you are tuned in and aware of them, you will not be able to notice them. When tuned into our True-Self these clues become so obvious that it provides a feeling of ignorance having never noticed them before. For example, everybody has had an experience when they thought they shouldn't have done something. It could be as simple as carrying several objects a short distance. Your gut instinct tells you that you shouldn't overload yourself, yet you decide that it is possible and carry all the items at once anyway. The result may be that one item, or even all, fall to the floor. Gut instincts appear instantly. They are there to help us survive in this world. If we are ever in a situation that threatens our survival, our gut instincts kick in. There is no time for our ego to step in and filter through all the information previously processed, in an attempt to find a solution. Our True-Self exists, we just need to look within, be present, and give it a chance to shine through. It will happily guide us to safety and inner-peace; we just need to remember how to allow it access to our conscious mind.

We either act on our gut instincts or we allow our environmental-Self to examine any possible reactions. The time spent examining, in a life threatening situation, is usually guided by our egoic mind, the part of the mind that goes through previous lessons that we have learned, or have been taught. The most likely outcome will be positive if you trust your first instinctive reactions, however, if you begin to examine all possibilities with your egoic mind, the outcome will most likely be negative or at least have negative influences over further related issues.

This egoic thinking process is what happens when suffering depression. The mind circles negative thoughts at such a rate that it becomes difficult to break free of them. Some thoughts may include "I am not worthy; everything I do is wrong" etc. These thoughts begin repeating themselves in our own mind until we become deaf to anything else, it as if we are programming ourselves to believe that we are not worthy. Any task that is attempted during this period, of egoic thinking, becomes a disaster, exhausting, and frustrating, which gives more fuel to continuing this type of negative thinking. These are not True-Self thoughts, but instead thoughts that are linked to external influences. Why would anybody think that they were overweight, unless magazines, newspapers, and television had managed to convince us that being overweight was bad? A foundation might be health, yet we still hear stories that extremely healthy people died of a sudden heart attack at a young age. If running ten miles a day made you healthy, then how could a person who does this die suddenly of a heart attack?

By studying ourselves, the way our own mind behaves, we gain an opportunity to do our own scientific research. This type of research has personal meaning because the proof has come from our own lives. Have you ever told someone something that wasn't true? Is it possible that many things we have been taught are not always correct? Take children's clothes for example. The younger they are the more likely their clothes are labelled with their age. The label may say '0–3 months', but that doesn't mean that your baby will fit into them when they are that age. You might have a smaller baby that can fit into this size when they are four or even five months old. If you had a very tall three month old baby they may only fit comfortably into clothing labelled '6–12 months'. It would seem strange to try and force a baby into sizes labelled with their actual age if they were obviously not going to fit into them. Anyone who has had a baby knows that when they are uncomfortable, they cry and scream. Most parents want their babies to be comfortable and happy. As we grow older, however we may follow fashionable advice and wear uncomfortable clothing, because we believe it makes us more socially acceptable. Even though the majority of the day may be spent adjusting uncomfortable clothing, many believe they are a better person or have more friends for being fashionable. Our True-Self eventually triumphs at the end of the day when we change out of uncomfortable clothes and relax in more comfortable attire.

There are many things that individuals suffer in order to comply with their environmental-Self. For women makeup is a huge crutch. The extreme individuals have become so dependent on makeup that they may even wear it while they sleep, or consider more permanent, surgical options. Women have been subject to large amounts of advertising with regards to makeup, many to the point where hiding behind a makeup mask is the only way they feel comfortable being in public. Our True-Self knows that this concept is insane; it knows that women don't need to wear makeup to be productive or successful, yet few have the inner strength to brave the world without makeup. We are told all these products are safe to use on our skin, but are they really? The skin is the biggest organ on the body, it needs access to oxygen. Our skin is porous, what we put on it can seep deeper. Is there any relation to the chemicals in sun cream and the formation of skin cancer? Few people question sun cream being a toxic substance, yet the ingredients are filled with chemicals that are produced in a laboratory and unpronounceable. For men there may be the issue of baldness. The majority of women don't really care if their partner is going bald. While many men prefer to see their women without makeup, let alone waiting for their partner to apply this makeup. These are many examples of how far we have distanced ourselves from our True-Self and when we begin to question our own preferences and reactions we can see that these are just the tip of the iceberg.

There is a True-Self within every individual. Some may be more tuned in and others may need more effort to connect with it, but we have all experienced direct connections at some point in our lifetimes. The more our environmental-Self has learned, the farther we are from our True-Self. When we are born, we know what makes us happy, we know that we need milk to drink when we are hungry and we make sure who ever is caring for us knows that we are hungry. As we grow older we have more responsibilities, we put off eating until we have accomplished certain tasks. We still know that we are hungry; we just ignore or distract ourselves by focusing on an activity. Unfortunately even our hunger can be manipulated by our environmental-Self through routine. We can have breakfast every day at 7am and if we miss it by a few hours our stomach is grumbling and moaning at us. There are many habits that we pick up throughout our lives and most of them have been shaped by our environment rather than from within us.

Our True-Self is all about our own truth. What is true for one may not be true for another and this is OK. What makes us happy may not make another happy. If it rains outside, you may believe it to be a miserable day, yet the plants, if dehydrated, may think it is a wonderful day. Our perspective is different to the plant. Humans think that because it is raining they are restricted, have to wear rain jackets, yet we feel refreshed when we have a shower or bath. Is it possible that the plants feel refreshed when it rains? If the plants feel good when it rains, then why do we feel bad? When children go out to play and get muddy and drag the mud into the house leaving mounds of clothes to be washed, the parents realise their chores have just increased. Yet the child did not think of this when they were playing happily with their friends. Instead they were having a brilliant time, throwing mud at each other. For a moment, if adults could realise that their child's playing ignited a sense of pleasure, excitement and encouraged the child to be creative by building dams and forts, then the extra chores of cleaning would become worthwhile. Yet the parent's perspective only sees the mess rather than the creativeness that occurred. We only see one perspective.

Perspective is not the only obstacle to overcome when moving towards living more instinctively. One must also become very aware of what they say or do. As the majority of people rely on information they have been previously given, can we even be certain that this information is true? History is usually written by the victorious side. Why would anyone want to hold up their hand to a mistake they made? Instead if we choose to learn from that mistake it becomes a valuable experience. How can all historic information be truthful when it is written in one perspective. That perspective may not convey the truth that applies to you. When repeating any information that we have been taught, how can we confirm that it is the truth? In science, the only way to prove something is to do the experiment yourself and view the results with your own eyes. That is the beauty of learning how to connect with your True-Self. You need to do it for yourself. It is a journey, an experience, something that you can observe, test, and improve from.

In our lifetime we can name many instances where someone told us something and it turned out to be untrue. I was once told by a school teacher 'you will never pass this exam.' Until this day I don't know if this was a psychological game that the teacher was playing, but the statement made me study harder and I passed that exam with flying colours. In this case the statement turned out to be untrue. I knew within myself that this was a warning and that if I didn't study harder, the teacher may turn out to be correct.

When connected with our True-Self, it is possible to read the world around us with a deeper level of understanding. Our True-Self works on an energetic level or vibrational frequency. This energy/frequency can be received, read and does not lie. Have you ever been asked how you are feeling today only to respond with "I'm fine thank you" even though you were not? Everybody has the ability to read into your untruthful response and feel that you are not OK, but with many people this particular situation just becomes a formality. We are conditioned to say we are 'fine' even when we are not. We are conditioned not to burden the other people with our personal problems. Usually our closest friends can tell when we express untruths and will delve into the issues at hand. This is because they care about us, they can read our frequency, and know whether we are telling the truth or not. They have practice in reading your vibrational frequency and have built confidence in knowing when and how to offer support. This is working with your True-Self and it may be a recognisable trait of your own.

When we are connected with our True-Self it is easy to read other people's frequency if you know them or not. It is even possible to hear these frequencies over the phone, where we are unable to see the person we are talking to, it may even be the case that we have never even met them. When learning to read these frequencies it is easiest to start with ourselves. Once these frequencies are observed they can then be controlled.

Anyone who has driven a car for a while has encountered a time when someone has dangerously overtaken them. This action usually results in feelings making us angry, causing us to think that the other driver was irresponsible, or it can cause us to become aggressive, urging us to drive really closely behind to annoy the other driver. Either way these feelings of anger and aggressiveness have been caused by an external stimulus, the other driver. We didn't intend to feel these negative emotions when we began our car journey, but we do have the option to allow these negative emotions to continue throughout the journey. That one event may influence the course of our day if we allow it to. Everything we encounter throughout that day has the ability to circle in our minds and dictate future events. It is ourselves that allow circling thoughts to continue. It is ourselves that can decide to dismiss circling thoughts as a waste of energy and move onto more positive thoughts. Some circling thoughts can be harder to dismiss than others. Just by saying the word 'cancel' or the statement 'this thought is a waste of energy' can help remove unwanted thoughts. The more committed we become to this practice, the quicker its effect. The end goal is encouraging happy thoughts which will lead to a happier day.

When we are connected with our True-Self, the external goings on in life have an effect, but it is short lived because a deeper level of peace and happiness is felt from within. External influences are noticed, but they do not have the strength to govern our lives more than deemed necessary. When we observe ourselves, by noticing our emotions and feelings, we can see how they are manipulated. In this way we are moving away from our environmental-Self and towards our True-Self. This movement is within the mind, within the levels of consciousness. It is acknowledging and taking control of how we perceive the world around us.

Believe it or not, the majority of people have experienced being connected to deeper levels of consciousness. Bonnie Christian in her article "What is Love?" interviews a neuroscientist who explains that Love emerges from the depths of our subconscious. "Our subconscious mind has about ten times more information than our rational brain...So when we actually fall in love with a person...the brain is working really hard to compute and to produce that feeling" (qtd.

n.p.). In this way "it's a complex series of computations of the subconscious brain that gives us an emotional experience we can't control" (n.p.). This is proof that our conscious mind has an existing connection with our subconscious mind and most likely even deeper levels than that. If our subconscious mind has ten times more information than our conscious mind, then deeper levels can potentially contain infinite levels of information. This could explain the strain accompanying NDE's as the brain attempts to process an influx of information received from deeper levels within their mind.

If love is a subconscious emotion, then when we feel it, we are working beyond the limits of our rational mind. When in love, we become filled with positive and loving feelings and have a tendency to idolize that which we are in love with. These positive, higher, vibrations open the gates to accessing the deeper levels of our mind, which in turn fill us with creativity and happiness. The deeper we travel within our mind, the closer we get to our Pure Mind, which is filled with Divine love. So when it is imagined that it is possible to reach Divine love, we are practicing a skill and increasing our ability to do so. The more we believe this skill exists, the more we become aware of it. When focused on the negative feelings of jealousy and hatred, we are closing the gates to the deeper levels of the mind, restricting ourselves to analytical thinking, and not processing information. We are limiting ourselves to what our environment can give us. This stagnation causes us to be stuck in the rational level of the mind. As human beings, we were given abilities above and beyond our conscious mind and it is our mission to learn to use them. Happiness comes through learning new skills; success comes through applying these new skills. Belief in obtaining new skills becomes the foundation. The question is, do you have the determination to become a happier person? There are many routines in our lives; can you make a conscious decision to improve your life using a new routine?

"The Truth that man should live by, states that you are essentially Pure, Divine, and Universal, through the Presence of God, your Creator, abiding within you" (Bachelor's Degree Curriculum, p. 3: 61). Ram Dass, in his book *Journey of Awakening*, describes what it feels like to be connected to the Creator by saying; "When you are in love with God, the very sound of the Name brings great joy. It is said that in its highest aspect, Divine Love is nothing less than the immortal bliss of liberation" (p. 71). He uses examples of many paths to obtain "deeper levels of opening and understanding" (p. 71), such as concentration, mantras, contemplation and devotion.

Whichever path is chosen will require persistence and that path can be switched at any time. Dass expresses that the final step in bringing the deeper levels to the surface of the mind "are [in the] ways of perceiving the world and the way you live in it such that each experience brings you more deeply into a meditative space" (p. 92). This continual connection with God seems to be the goal of most 'Spiritual' human beings and those whom achieve it seem to use it within every possible moment of their lives.

Levels of Consciousness

So what is our higher consciousness, or interconnectedness with the Universe and Nature? Caroline Hindle lists, *10 Levels of Consciousness*, in her article. She states that within the first level of consciousness "You are an embodiment of your external environment, with all its positive and negative aspects" (p. n.p.). In this level you are only aware of your environmental-Self. Society and its programming's are all you understand, it is the only truth you know and how you define your personality. Hindle describes money and consumerism as the two main factors that govern your emotions. If you have a nice car and smart clothes, you will feel more successful. It is for this reason that we initially discussed the effects that Western Civilization has on us. Things are taken very personally, if someone is aggressive towards you, you counter it by being the victim. This level of consciousness is mostly run in an auto-pilot manner where little intuitive thinking or responses happen. If it is believed that everything you have been told is the truth, you are limiting yourself to the lowest level of consciousness. Here you believe that the media, teachers, and doctors never lie and always provide truthful information.

Hindle describes the second level as the beginning of looking inwards. If you have never examined your feelings or spent time considering how to react before, then just by reading this book you have achieved the second level of consciousness. Within this level you are drawn to examining the effects that the world around you has. The controlling ability of individuals becomes clearer in the everyday people you meet. As you begin to realise this, you begin to take back control of yourself. Your need to follow the masses diminishes and instead you begin to find the inner strength needed to research, understand, and stand up for what you believe in. The fear of breaking away and going your own way starts to diminish, even if it is against other people's advice.

This is because your own, deeper ability to 'know' what serves your Higher-Self increases and takes control overpowering your environmental-Self. The urge to change your circle of friends creeps in as you choose to associate yourself with more like minded people, those who match or increase your vibration. Your need for drama diminishes and you find yourself spending time with more positive people rather than negative ones who thrive on gossip and belittling others.

The transformation from the first level of consciousness to the second level can be confusing and frustrating, but it always ends up empowering. Everything you have previously thought to be the truth requires questioning. It becomes possible to notice that your favourite television programs are full of drama which has subconsciously programmed you to believe that similar drama is required in your own relationships. This part of the transformation urges you to shy away from starting drama, as you begin to distance yourself from those that relish in it. More and more of society are beginning to experience this shift from the environmental-Self to the True-Self and because their results are positive they are encouraging others to do the same. Our purpose in this world is to evolve and eventually all will experience each level of consciousness. Some have many more lessons to learn before they choose to make the decision to evolve and this is part of their own journey. There is no need to rush others; there is only a need to continue to self-evolve.

Hindle states that in the third level, "you become more sensitive" (p. n.p.). The 'knowing' feeling inside becomes stronger. This stage becomes a purging of your emotions. Many emotions have been bottled up, deep inside, for a while and now they begin to surface. You may not be aware of the emotion that has been stored away, although it will become more difficult not to let your emotions out. All buried emotions become unlocked and you may become angry without cause, or cry without reason, as you release emotionally charged energy. The emotions will swing rapidly as they float up and out of your energy field. One moment you can be happy and the next you may break down in tears. Your mind may associate these emotions with memories or things that are happening in your environment. Here you begin to break the links of unnecessary stimuli plus emotion connections that no longer serve you in a higher vibrational lifestyle. It is at this time where the 'tree hugger' inside you emerges. You will find that in nature, you can let all these emotions out. Nature is there to nurture and will help clear you of stagnant emotional energies. The feeling of the earth on your skin will also help during this process as its energy will calm you. Children and animals become more inquisitive about you and you become better at reading their emotions. Your empathetic abilities increase as you feel more emotions of the people around you. Their emotions can often be mistaken for your own as you still have a very individual mind set. The energy of others easily transfers to you, although your ability to determine your own emotions is increasing. Here it is important to become the watcher of your emotions. Allow them to flow through you. Watch them come and watch them go. Question any associations with these emotions and the current situations in your life. The longer we suppress, or ignore, these emotions, the stronger they become and more likely they are to return. Allowing them to flow freely, not to get caught up in them, will help them pass through faster. We must understand that human beings naturally have emotions; in the spiritual world these emotions are very powerful. At this stage the more we acknowledge these emotions, the more we create a new library of how we feel when experiencing them. This library of feelings will become very important when travelling through the deeper levels of consciousness as they add urgency to the creative forces. This level of consciousness is splattered with moments of inner peace. Moments where you feel no need to change anything as your appreciation for what you are increases.

The fourth level of consciousness is where you emerge "as an individual and begin to take an active role in your life" (Hindle, 2016). This is the level where you begin to value time, where every moment becomes precious. Wasting time is not using time wisely as you are creating nothing, or the wrong things. In order to move from an auto-pilot life, you begin to use your time wisely, plan, and set the foundations for you new and improved life. A life that is more centred on becoming happy as you begin to realise that to make others happy, you yourself must *first* be happy. You gain the realization that time turns into a series of consciously aware *now* moments. The power to change your thoughts in this *now* moment will have an effect on what happens later. You begin to become conscious of the random thoughts that spin around in your head, some good, some bad. Using this awareness you gain the ability to control the randomness of thoughts. Conscious decisions become focused on the nice, positive, thoughts and are then further built on. You become more imaginative and creative. Any negative thoughts get thrown away instantly as they serve no purpose and it is realized they are a waste of your valuable time. You may even speak or think the word *cancel* when you have a negative thought as this helps nullify it. During the fourth level of consciousness you truly comprehend if the people around you are helping or hindering you.

In the fifth level of consciousness "you treat your body and mind with respect and maintain harmony and balance through your daily regimen" (Hindle, 2016). With the realisation of what served you in the previous stages, this is the stage where you begin to take the actions necessary to preserve your state of well being. Now you begin to truly feel the positive effects of knowing yourself. You have done what you need to clear stagnant emotions, you associate more so with others who bring positive vibrations, and you have eliminated the unnecessary tasks in your life. It is as if you are coming out of the cocoon and emerging a butterfly. Your new found wings give you the ability to sail over what used to bring you down. Negative comments from others show the truth of how they themselves are hurting and noticing this takes the negative impact away from you personally. You begin to see the meaning in everyday situations, that they are meant to teach valuable lessons and your association with their negative emotional ties disappear. You look back on your regrets and notice the valuable lessons you learned and then they no longer weigh you down as regrets. These previous events happened for a reason, to shape you into who you are now, if they didn't occur, you would be a different person. A sense of success fills you as you realise the life you have now is the best life you could have wished for. With this knowledge you choose to create an even better life going forward. You no longer do things because you are forced; you do them because you decide to. Even the little chores that used to cause frustration become projected with love so that others unknowingly receive this love.

Moving to the sixth stage of consciousness, "you are in the world but you no longer feel part of it" (Hindle, 2016). Your world becomes one of energy rather than one of form. You understand that if you touch a block of metal, you have an effect on it. This effect may be microscopic, but it is an effect none the less. You visualize your energy as if it is a drop of food dye in a bowl of water, spreading to each part within the bowl, within your environment. You are now fully in control of how your energy affects others and you begin to use this ability to help others.

Just one smile, greeting a stranger has the ability to lift their whole day. The situations in your daily life motivate playful contemplation, as if each situation is a puzzle to figure out. More information that is gathered, the more you require to digest and examine it. An understanding of something greater than you begins to emerge. You move from knowing yourself to wanting to know this higher energy. This urge to know, leads you to research more until you find that information pops out at you. Relevant books, articles, and experiences all seem to appear and show themselves at the right point in your learning process. Coincidences occur far too often to be considered as chance; instead they become signs to follow. Externally you give off the impression that you have it all together and others become drawn to you and ask for advice in their own lives.

As we move upwards through the levels, the aspects of being an individual merge into the aim of becoming a part of a whole and connecting with whatever it is that encompasses that whole. In the seventh level of consciousness you begin to, "understand what lies in the hearts of people, you feel their pain and know how to heal them" (Hindle, 2016). Those who come to you with their issues miraculously find solutions in a short period of time. It is as if your acknowledgement of their issues has reached a spiritual collective which then manifests solutions. Your heart has become warmed by the Higher Power you have been searching for; this warmth can be felt physically. It is a warmth that can be switched on whenever it is required and comes from a connection with your own soul. You hold a sense of peace, a knowing that the bigger picture is positively manifesting in front of your very own eyes. You gain the confidence that every word, every action, that is made is for the good of all human kind. You shift from improving yourself to improving the energies of your environment. You realise that all form, all life, is made up of energy in constant motion, in this way you understand your fluid connection with everything around you. A Higher Power has so much influence over you that you ooze love for everyone, everything, and every situation. It is as though you become a servant to this Higher Power and your only goal is to spread love and heal others. The necessity to judge others is lost as you realise they have their own reasoning behind their actions. This reasoning is a part of their journey which in itself is a beautiful thing to observe. Everyone has their own journey and their own lessons to learn. It becomes obvious if your input into these journeys is required and you are happy even if it is not. You can see no wrong decisions and you become light hearted when others take large amounts of time over minimal impact decisions.

In the next level of consciousness, the eighth level, "the barriers between your ego and the collective are beginning to crumble" (Hindle, 2016). Your mission is now fully under a Higher Power. You find the strength to fight for the rights of all humanity. You know that meditations can be guided with affirmations which have an impact on the Collective Mind. This information can then be fed back to all humanity through their individual subconscious connections. All your intentions are of the purest vibration and therefore only provide positivity. Your understanding of manipulating energy is expressed through raising the vibration of yourself and others. For this you need no reward as your reward is your connection to a Higher Power. You need no acknowledgement for you efforts. Your every thought has an influence and you use these to create a reality that is pure and good. Any who disagree with you soon become transparent, they have no impact on you as your only guide is a Higher Power, an Infinite Power that cannot be suppressed by any force. You understand that this Higher Power is worshiped by many and goes by many names, all of which are valid. You know that this Higher Power is purity itself and has no need to harm, no need to punish. You may begin to question some of the lessons in ancient and newer religions, as your connection may make you aware of some inaccuracies. Here again, you know yourself through a Higher Power and what is right for you is acknowledged that it might not be right for others. For this you have respect for those who stand up for their own rights and accept a difference of opinions. There is no need for opposition; there is only a need for adoration of others' truth. Love becomes the only emotion or feeling required.

This feeling of love spreads from within you in the ninth level of consciousness where "your mind, heart, spirit, body, and soul are one" (Hindle, 2016). You are now working with all the gifts given to you. Your heart is connected to a Higher Spirit, your soul is guiding your path, and your mind is adapting this information to aid you in this physical world of form. Your body becomes a vessel that is making this transfer of information possible to other vessels. When previously looking at the physics behind the electrical and chemical manipulation of information throughout the body-system, it was discussed that if one part of the body-system fails, the whole system fails. In the ninth level of consciousness you are working as a whole, spiritually and physically. One system comprised of body, mind, spirit and soul, all working together. It is still possible to function in the world, although the world seems the brightest it has ever been. It becomes nearly impossible to see fault in anything. It is as though you can see the final result of all situations so there is no need to concern yourself with anything other than creating more love in the world. The love that you naturally project welcome's and comforts other life around you, you may even find plants grow bigger and flower more if kept around you. The worries of income seem distant and unnecessary memories as you realise that these worries are manifesting into negative financial situations. Instead you focus on the opportunities that come your way and use your instinctive and creative skills towards them. The results from living this way provide financial stability, a sense of success, deep inner peace, and blissful happiness.

In the tenth level of consciousness "you have become fused with the collective" (Hindle, 2016). Your ability to manifest your desires becomes limitless. The point to remember at this level of consciousness is that your old, egoic desires, no longer exist. There is no need to prove yourself to others, as you have no need to impress anyone. Material goods no longer serve as things that make you happy or sad. Instead they are just seen as part of the collective creative forces. There is no wrong or right; only lower or higher vibrational levels. As you are love itself, you see the lack of love in others and wish to help them as you know that they are a part of you. Everything in your world is a part of you and you want to raise the vibration of it all. You are fully capable of helping people when they are around you or when they are not. The concept of time and space are constructs of the physical world and hold little influence over spiritual energy transfer.

This is a generalization of the levels of consciousness. As an individual you may notice more specific details that fall under some of the descriptions. I encourage you to examine as much of your daily life as possible and notice how you feel. Try and think if it is possible to change your reaction and increase it through the levels of consciousness. Throughout the day we travel through these levels, back and forth. It is as though we have a passport and can easily move from one level to another. Sometimes we may get caught up in the aspects of daily living that may drag us down towards the lower egoic levels, but this is possible to change, through the use of the mind. We have the ability to change our perspective and hence achieve the higher, more divine, levels. For example, when going for a job interview, you might become anxious, worry about not being able to financially support your family if you don't get the position. This is the first egoic level of thinking. It is easy, once practiced, to change your perspective by understanding that if this job is the right one for you, then the energy will be there and you will get it. By doing this the worries and stresses become dulled and replaced with excitement about the possibility of a new path in life. An opportunity to meet new people, hear their stories and learn from them. You will also gain new skills that could help in other activities you enjoy.

Energy is never motionless and when living as a human being on earth, each level of consciousness has its purpose, so it is necessary to travel between levels. One way of thinking of it is that the Collective Mind is a library and we are gathering experiences to record into this library. The library itself does not know good or bad, all it knows is the emotion that you attached to your experience. If you focus on positive experiences and disregard the negative ones, your section of the library will become a positive one. When you are focused on the positive, you need to go out of your way to get to the section where the negative books are stored in the library. It becomes wasted energy go to an entirely different section to find negative books, so you stay in the positive section. The positive books are closer to hand and by sticking with them you will be subject to more positive experiences in life.

Finding our True-Self

Are these states of spiritual evolvement, vibrational levels or abilities only allowed to be experienced by priests, mystics, Shamans and Buddha's? In Dr. Masters *Ministers/Bachelor's Degree Modules*, he teaches "how to use the EXACT SAME POWER that Christ and other beings utilized down through the ages-a power to which the so-called "Supernatural" was attributed" (p. 1: 1). He states that this "absolute power is available to all human beings" (p. 1: 1) and it is defined as finding one's relationship with their own mind and the Universe. A "Supreme Universal Mind" (p. 1: 2) lies within the deeper levels of our own mind and we can learn the ability to make direct contact with it. Figure 8 is a visual representation Dr. Masters uses to show how the Universal Mind lies within our own mind. Our consciousness is directly connected to our personal subconscious while the Universal Mind, or Pure-Mind, lies at the deepest level of the mind. Conscious contact with the Pure Mind allows us to receive guidance, which once acted upon, will have the effect of improving our daily life. This connection is achieved by learning how to synthesize the functional, conscious mind with the Pure Mind (Masters P. L., Bachelor's Degree Curriculum, p. 1: 2).

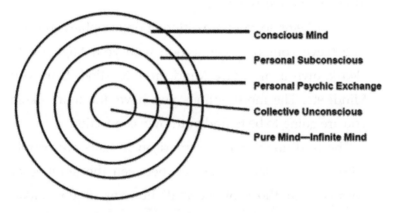

Conscious Mind

Personal Subconscious

Personal Psychic Exchange

Collective Unconscious

Pure Mind—Infinite Mind

Figure 8. Masters, Paul Leon. Master's Degree Modules. (1: 12)

Don Juan uses the term *nagual* in his description of where the power hovers, which can be compared to the deep felt knowing mystics have when they are in contact with God. Although mystics sense this knowingness, it cannot be explained to others through descriptions understandable by the senses. I see the only scientific proof being one of personal experience. Mystics use meditation to digest the information that comes from their senses in order to gain knowledge to heal themselves, others, and everything around them.

Their lives are led perusing avenues which strengthen their connection to the deeper levels within themselves, while the goal is being able to connect with God or their own form of a Higher Power. Animals have a stronger instinctive-nature, shown through their ability to sense illnesses and earthquakes.

Let us begin to compare different philosophies on ways to achieve your own connection with your Higher-Self, also known as the Pure Mind, Infinite Mind, Universal Mind, etc. The more options you have, the more likely you are going to be to find your own connection.

The traditional Native American Indians are people who seem to bridge the gap between the abilities of animals and those of 'normal' humans. Bobby Lake-Thom is of this origin and uses his skills as a healer and spiritual teacher. In his book, *Spirits of the Earth*, he says that today's society is desensitizing itself, favouring rational thinking over intuitive thinking. As most modern people do not understand how to communicate with Nature, they fear the knowledge gained from it. They try discrediting and ignoring this knowledge by using terms like 'supernatural' and 'superstitious' (p. 10). Lake-Thom has been through Western education, gaining a Masters' degree. He says he has learned to psychically switch between both sides of his mind-brain complex (p. 12). In other words he has mastered the ability to use different levels of consciousness, moving from the egoic world of form to the spiritual world of energies. He says that "most people are never taught how to use the unconscious, the intuitive-spiritual side of the brain" (p. 13). Lake-Thom describes the term 'mind-brain complex' as being made up of six parts (see Figure 9). The 'conscious left brain hemisphere' is objective, logical, science and technology orientated, while the 'conscious right brain hemisphere' is driven through the five senses, physically orientated, and controls motor skills. There are many people in this world who limit themselves to only using this part of the brain. These are people who are heavily orientated towards their environmental-Self, they are more inclined to believe and do what they are told. When we limit ourselves to only the conscious abilities, there is little inspirational creativity and/or scientific breakthroughs. The unconscious part of our brain is split into four parts, the 'male', which holds information from parents and relatives, and the 'female' which is spiritually orientated, including psychic powers and a sixth sense. The male part will be linked to hereditary information while the female part will be linked with extrasensory information. The remaining two parts of the unconscious mind include the 'Anima' which understands spirits, forces and powers in the mind from Nature, and 'Animus' which is affected by myths, dreams, imagination, rituals, visions and spiritual experiences (p. 45). When we study each encounter with our external world, we should try to use each part of our mind-brain complex. By doing this it is possible to gain a perception which is equally balanced, both physically and spiritually. When we limit ourselves to only using the logical, 'conscious left brain hemisphere', we are shutting the passage, restricting further information from being received and therefore desensitizing our ability to process this information.

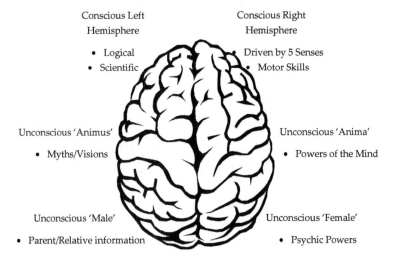

Conscious Left
Hemisphere
- Logical
- Scientific

Conscious Right
Hemisphere
Driven by 5 Senses
Motor Skills

Unconscious 'Animus'
- Myths/Visions

Unconscious 'Anima'
- Powers of the Mind

Unconscious 'Male'
- Parent/Relative information

Unconscious 'Female'
- Psychic Powers

Figure 9. Mind-Brain Complex

118

Lake-Thom expresses the importance of using the senses to pick up information from the Earth, plants, and animals, as they have much to teach us. "The powers from Nature may be demonstrated or perceived for that they really are, in the form of all those who walk, crawl, fly, and swim-in other words, what traditional American Indian people call 'all our relations'" (p. 196). Their teachings say that as human beings, we are "part of the great web of life [which] makes us all part of Nature. We are influenced and affected by Nature, and we in turn directly influence and affect Nature" (p. 196). Native American Indians have a great amount of respect for Nature stating that "everything is a source of 'power'" (p. 8) and that everything in Nature has a spirit of its own and thus a connection to the Great Spirit. The term 'Great Spirit' is sometimes replaced with other terms such as God, the "Great Creator, the Maker, the Great Mystery, or the Great Invisible One" (p. 7). Their belief system teaches them to worship the Great Spirit as well as to respect and communicate "with that which God has created...They see the life-giving force of the Great Spirit flowing through all things in the Universe" (p. 7). To gain knowledge, sources of power, protection and supernatural aids, they "communicate through praying, talking, singing, dancing, meditating, touching, smelling, and/or offering tobacco, herbal smoke, food, or some other gift to one of their relations" (p. 8). Rituals, ceremonies, myths, and stories play an important role in passing down valuable knowledge to future generations. This knowledge brings an understanding of how to communicate with Nature as well as ways of overcoming fear and effectively dealing with any life situation as it arises (p. 35).

Native American Indians are encouraged to experience these teachings and lessons for themselves. Part of Lake-Thom's personal training required his commitment and discipline to spend many hours outside studying different birds in their natural habitat. He was asked to recite what "color they were, how they behaved among themselves and with the other birds, and how they related to other creatures and their natural environment" (p. 26). This training heightened his own sensitivity, awareness, and his ability to understand Nature and all its symbols. He never recorded his experiences, instead, stored them in his subconscious by meditating upon them "to explore the unconscious part of … [his] mind-brain complex" (p. 27) in order to "synthesize the conscious and unconscious" (p. 46). This process allows one to gain supernatural powers which aid in allowing one "to survive, adapt, and succeed in life" (p. 49). Taking the time to mentally process what we experience, either physically or spiritually, heightens our physical and spiritual abilities. This processing time is one of the many forms of meditation. All it requires is conscious thought about what you experienced. Keeping your mind focused is the key to your own success.

The traditional American Indian believes nothing is a coincidence, that every life situation has a lesson to teach us and when we use both hemispheres of our mind-brain complex we can begin to learn, for ourselves, how to evolve as a result of these lessons (Lake-Thom, p. 51). Their goal is to find, within oneself, interconnectedness with all things in Nature and the Universe. Certain powers such as telepathic communication, our "original language" (Lake-Thom, p. 59), are considered to help find one's own union with the Great Spirit. Often drawn circles in the dirt are sat within, as circles are symbols that act as 'connectors' to powers while prayer can be used to activate these powers within (Lake-Thom, p. 37).

Names from Nature such as Crazy Horse or Sitting Bull are earned and believed to "serve as... passport[s] to the Great Creator and the spirit world" (Lake-Thom, p. 39). One can earn their own "secret name from Nature via meditation, vision-seeking, or through a prayer request or dream" (Lake-Thom, p. 40). "The 'traditional'

Native Americans ...see the world as a great mystery, full of magic, mysticism, challenge, and liveliness" (Lake-Thom, p. 189). They respect everything, in both the physical and spiritual terms, while soaking up as much information as possible in order to transform it into forms that benefit their own physical and spiritual evolvement.

Another view point from a Yaqui Indian from Sonora, Mexico can be found in Carlos Castaneda's book, *Tales of Power*. Castaneda is the apprentice of Don Juan who trains Castaneda to be a warrior through educating him in the traits of impeccability, humbleness and knowingness. Don Juan describes humans as a feeling inside a body of luminous fibres that have awareness (p. 94). He says "that it was not so difficult to let the spirit of a man flow and take over; to sustain it, however, was something that only a warrior could do" (p. 110). In this way, a warrior is someone willing to persist in their path towards awakening. Anyone can be a warrior; all it takes is a determination to follow it through. This is the case with any skill; it takes practice and dedication to improve.

In his training, Don Juan uses the theory that at the moment of birth we have two sides, personal to each of us, that become operative. He terms these two sides as the *tonal* and the *nagual*. Although similar to conscious and unconscious parts of the mind, the *tonal* and the *nagual* is another interesting concept to consider. The *tonal* is described as a "...kind of guardian spirit, usually an animal..." with which we have intimate ties with for the rest of our lives (Castaneda, p. 119). The *nagual* is "...the name given to the animal into which sorcerers could allegedly transform themselves" (Castaneda, p. 119). Don Juan further describes the *tonal* as "...our organizer...everything we know and do as men is the work of the *tonal*" (Castaneda, p. 120). It is everything that meets the eye and every grasp of air from the moment of birth to the end at death. He discusses this theory with Castaneda at a restaurant, comparing the *tonal* to an island where he uses the table in front of them to represent the island. Everything that Castaneda could label with a name, could be represented by something placed on the table and therefore a part of our *tonal*. Castaneda begins naming things that he thinks would be the *nagual*; the mind, the soul, thoughts, Heaven, psyche, and vital forces. For each item named, Don Juan puts something physical on the table, such as a napkin, an ashtray, silverware, etc. until the table is piled high with items. Getting frustrated, Castaneda asks if God is the *nagual*. Don Juan responds with "No.

God is only everything you can think of, therefore, properly speaking, he is only another item on the island. God cannot be witnessed at will; he can only be talked about. The *nagual*, on the other hand, is at the service of the warrior. It can be witnessed, but it cannot be talked about" (Castaneda, p. 125). "The *nagual* is the part of us which we do not deal with at all...for which there is no description – no words, no names, no feelings, no knowledge" (Castaneda, p. 124). Don Juan then states 'the *nagual*...is surrounding the island...where the power hovers." (Castaneda, p. 126). The *nagual* is beyond the comprehension of our senses. We can reach the *nagual*, although it is only recognized as fleeting glances. Because our senses cannot decipher information from the *nagual*, it is received consciously as flashes, moments of inspiration, recalled dreams, all of which are aspects that cannot be explained by the senses. Instead these fleeting glances come as soul-felt knowingness from within. Our *tonal* cannot explain this information by means of the senses, as a result we tend to disregard it as insanity or try to use our reason to explain these things to ourselves, at which point we lose the messages and our reason, or functional mind, has won.

In Figure 8 it is shown that our conscious mind is the outside circle, the most readily accessed level of consciousness. When Don Juan describes the *nagual*, it can be compared to the Pure Mind, the innermost circle. Carl G. Jung, in his book, *The Archetypes and the Collective Unconscious*, adds further weight to the idea of a Pure Mind when he states that within each of us "exists a second psychic system of a collective, universal, and impersonal nature which is identical in all individuals" (p. 43). Jung describes the great goal in life is that of achieving a connection with this higher consciousness, the very same goal of all mystics.

Who are mystics and how have they learned their skills? In Marsha Sinetar's book, *Ordinary People as Monks & Mystics*, she interviews many people who have risen "up against some aspect of a false self [the ego] that whispers they can't fulfil their sensed, most noble purposes" (p. xvi). She describes monks and mystics as individuals who have gained the confidence in living a life of faith and have surrendered their fear in abiding to the social pressures within society. A new clarity within life is achieved including a "soundness of mind" (p. xvii), which comes as a result of consciously integrating their inner and outer realities (p. 1). In this way, Monks and Mystics have the ability to understand energies beyond those recognized by the five senses and know when information, taken in from the senses, is contradictive to what they know and feel inside themselves (p. 72). With this deeper perception, they can manipulate their own reality and *know* that eventually all experiences, good or bad, are for their evolvement. Their lives become an everlasting learning journey, filled with opportunities to find the next sign or signal. These signals become the building blocks towards understanding their part and purpose within this Universe. "The mystic's goal [is] to *be* in, and with God-not to have intellectual knowledge or special advantage over others" (p. 94). These individuals have found their connection with a higher consciousness and through that connection they gain ever increasing abilities which aid their lifelong evolutionary process. Their "fear of death dissolves" (p. 101) and is replaced with feelings of being reborn, becoming whole, and they have a noticeable determination to hold onto these feelings.

Sinetar states that "mystics can attain a highly developed cosmic sense" (p. 106), or connection to a higher consciousness. The benefits of this connection are that the ego, or environmental-Self, becomes a secondary advisor to their True-Self, leaving a "deeper, fuller identity" (p. 114) than that which can be achieved by the limited ego-Self. Individuals who are highly dependent on their ego can compare the experience of a diminishing ego during moments of orgasm where it is possible to transcend self-consciousness (Dass, p. 3). To achieve their connection to a higher consciousness, monks and mystics seem to go through a transformation which forces them to face up to and release their egoic, darker energies. This process is like a psychic rebirth, a "birth into a higher level of functioning, perceiving, [and] feeling" (Sinetar, p. 114). They gain the ability of being "keenly receptive to what is…as well as to what is superfluous or dishonest" (Sinetar, p. 135). Mystics learn to listen to their True-Self by becoming "self-referring, rather than other- or world-referring: progressively they design life from an intra-psyche perspective rather than from rules, idols and status symbols of society" (Sinetar, p. 170). In other words, they are true to their Divine or instinctive-Self and not bound by their environmental-Self, or ego.

The abilities and sensitivities of monks and mystics are not limited to them alone. "Anyone, of any age and background, can grow whole. One only needs a sincere heart and the purity and strength of intent to identify then express, what is discerned to be true and virtuous" (Sinetar, p. 138). Mystics connect with a higher consciousness and the skills required to obtain this connection can be learned and developed by anyone with the determination and faith to do so. It is the same as learning any musical instrument or language where willpower must be present. Effort needs to be focused towards a goal in order to achieve a result.

Sandra Ingerman, author of *Walking in Light: the Everyday Empowerment of a Shamanic Life*, gives us a further method of achieving higher states of consciousness through shamanic journeying. "The word *shaman* comes from the Tungus tribe in Siberia and means 'spiritual healer' or 'one who sees in the dark'" (p. xv). A shamanic journey will allow one to work with the "invisible worlds and formless energies" (p. xxi). There are specific routines to follow in order to have a successful journey and these routines form a ceremony. Ceremonies allow "humans to connect with the spiritual world and create a relationship and interaction between the visible and invisible realms" (p. 3). Each ceremony starts with creating a sacred space where one can set an intention, or something that one wishes to achieve from the journey. Sometimes wearing specific items of clothing, sitting on rugs or in certain areas are sufficient to create a sacred space. This is the time when one's focus is on joining together mind, body and spirit (p. 5). Sitting comfortably and taking deep breaths will help dissolve distracting thoughts (p. 1). Deep breathing and holding your hands over your heart can allow you to feel your heartbeat. Imagining that the Earth also has a heartbeat and matching the two beats together will bring a sense of connection with the Earth and Spirit of the Land. Shamans believe in helping spirits and allies, whom are welcomed at the start of a ceremony. The middle of the ceremony is where one concentrates on their intention and this can be done in many ways. Movement is encouraged during ceremonies, as it can help build energies with the helping spirits who have the ability to physically manifest desired outcomes. Some people dance, sing, or burn pieces of paper with their intention written on it (p. 7). It is suggested to be conscious of what the senses are picking up and using this information to further the journey. Whenever Ingerman hears a sound from her environment, she tells herself "every sound I hear takes me deeper into my journey – and it does" (p. 14). The closing stage of a ceremony involves "thanking the elements and all the spiritual forces that held you in love and witnessed your transformation and healing" (p. 7). "There is no right way to experience a shamanic journey" (p. 11). Instead variation in practice helps.

One can listen to drumming, bang sticks together, or shake a bottle with pebbles in it.

Ingerman states that everyone can learn to have the abilities of a shaman. They can shift "into an altered state of consciousness, a spiritual state of consciousness, to travel outside of time into the hidden realms that many people call non-ordinary reality" (Ingerman, p. 8). She asks us to refer to our childhood when we did it naturally by using our imaginations, had invisible friends, and even travelled to the stars. Using each moment to consciously become aware of the information our senses are attuned to, will bring us closer to our pure, luminous, divine-Self.

By now it will be becoming apparent that when we live through our environmental-Self, we limit the ability of our True-Self. It is also understood that our senses and abilities have been dulled down due to the society we live in, but what is the reason behind this desensitization or contamination? The Hermetica explains how an ancient Egyptian philosophy of life and its teachings, allowed normal people such as Buddha and Christ to become 'awakened', experience higher states of consciousness, and have mystical abilities. Was this information hidden from the masses, even in ancient Egyptian times, so that only the few could experience it? Matthew Barnes attempts to decipher the teachings of Hermes Trismegistus, also known as the Egyptian God Thoth, in his book *The Hermetica 101*. The Hermetica tell us "what creates life, what our purpose is here on earth and what is beyond this life" (p. 1). Many famous people such as "Leonardo da Vinci, Paracelsus, Shakespeare...Sir Isaac Newton [and] Sir Walter Raleigh" (p. 2) attribute their success to Hermetic teachings in their acknowledgment of finding the wisdom within to produce great works. The teachings encourage each individual to experience the truth for them self. This contradicted the beliefs of early Christian and Muslim churches who believed that the truth was only known, for certain, by priests. The churches promoted the idea that all, apart from priests, should become religious followers "required to blindly rely on that priest's guidance" (p. 3) as to what they should believe in and how they should act. Those who went against the beliefs of priests were persecuted and threatened with torture and death. With the threat against one's own survival, society succumbed to the belief that true wisdom can only be found in the lessons from the church. The Egyptians wanted their teachings to remain as personal journeys rather than a "dogmatic set of rules" (p. 3), so their 'awakening' journey to see "beyond the 'veil' of this world into the 'Soul of the Universe'" (p. 6) became a secretive journey. For this reason, "'hermetic' in modern terms, means 'sealed' [or] 'secret'" (p. 5).

I hold no religion in higher regards over any other. I do however question the concept that God is 'out there somewhere'. I have learned more about God, or a Higher Power, through my own individual studies by experiencing the different levels of consciousness. This method has shown me that a Higher Power is within me, it is within all of us. There can be no set instructions that will apply to everyone to enable them to find this Higher Power, as we are all on individual journeys. I agree with Barnes in that Hermetic teachings create an understanding of the world that "make us masters over our own lives" (The Hermetica 101, p. 4) and can only be understood by "those who were ready to hear them" (The Hermetica 101, p. 5). I believe every individual path of awakening encourages an understanding of what God is and shows us how to follow life's flow in order to reduce suffering.

Barnes states that this individual journey to God contradicted the churches beliefs by suggesting that 'normal' people could learn to connect with God and those who practiced it were treated as outcasts or even killed. As societal pressures increased people were influenced not to awaken for themselves causing individuals power to diminish and many were forced to follow the flow of society rather than their natural inner-flow. Barnes explains the resistance to life's natural flow by using the example of a naked and wet person going out in the snow, or a person stepping into one hundred degree weather in heavy winter attire. Both will result in a likely hood of getting sick. This illness is not a punishment by God, rather a person not understanding "the way things work, the way your body works, and [therefore they will have] suffered the natural consequences" (The Hermetica 101, p. 7).

The Hermetica encourages self-discovery through exploring, learning, and creating on a personal level. As children we are curious, while as adults, we are at our happiest when engaging in activities that lead to exciting discoveries (The Hermetica 101, p. 9). When Hermetic teachings are encouraged within society, such as the free-thinking Renaissance period, society flourishes through progression and learning. Arabic areas influenced by Hermetic teachings birthed "great astronomers, like Copernicus" (The Hermetica 101, p. 11). The people in these areas discovered sulphuric acid, geometry, algebra, and they learned how to make paper from cotton, linen and rags, invented mechanical clocks, worked with optics and "contributed greatly to medicine" (The Hermetica 101, p. 12). When Hermetic teachings are banned or suppressed, society enters Dark Ages (The Hermetica 101, p. 11).

In his book, Barnes explains that the Hermetica states that in order for one to 'awaken', they require a "knowledge [that] shines the light on Life" (p. 15). This knowledge allows one to "glimpse the immortality of the Mind..., Soul..., your Higher-Self..., [as well as] the Intelligence behind the scenes. Once you understand the rules of this world, you navigate it better. And once you see that you are not your body, that you go on after death, what could there be to harm you" (p. 15)? Hermes describes living "in a spiritual era where science and religion come together" (p. 23) and that their separation will occur in the future. "Religion is the study of God [and] science is the study of what God created" (p. 24). "Religion without science is ignorant and intolerant, while science without religion is lonely and smug" (p. 25). When will science begin to investigate the spiritual, or are these investigations that must be done on a personal level only?

Barnes translates Hermes Trismegistus describing a time when he was "deep in silence... [and his] mind was focused" (p. 27). During this time Hermes 'felt' an Intelligence speaking to him and saw a boundless Light of Consciousness, which he described as *IT*. "*IT* was Intelligence, *IT* was Science and *IT* was Religion" (p. 30) and he felt like he was 'home' within *IT*s presence. Hermes described *IT* as a vibration (p. 33), which was in continuous motion. *IT* told him that his body was governed by the Laws of Nature, but his mind, his consciousness, is free and "creates what it wills" (p. 37). The voice told Hermes "Consciousness is the miracle you seek... [and it] gives birth to creations" (p. 38). The body is heavy, from "the world of matter..., [but] his Consciousness, his Mind, [is] from his Father" (p. 40). The voice was telling Hermes that *IT* lies within his consciousness and that *IT* is The Father. Hermes begs with The Father to continue to live within its boundless light as he was eager to gain further knowledge. He was told that this is only done by consciously choosing to do so. Hermes was taught to understand that this world should be regarded as only a garment where attachment to material things is unnecessary and will only bring obsession and selfishness (p. 48). Instead Hermes should give up material attachments and be compassionate, creative, and love unconditionally as these are the things that bring happiness. Give without any reward of receiving, do not harm others or steal as those are dark deeds which will bring darkness and unhappiness (p. 49). Those whom "seek the Light, but have been tempted by the dark..., [believe the rewards are] easier to obtain and more immediately satisfying. But it is an illusion and once trapped within, it is hard to get out...It is a vicious cycle" (p. 50).

When we limit ourselves with our functional brain our focus is on the external, material world, rather than in the internal world. Attachment is the cause of suffering; it clouds the Watcher within "separating you [your ego] from your own Self and you live from your desires instead of from your Center" (The Hermetica 101, p. 53). When we are centered, we are able to 'watch' what our senses pick up from the outside world. When we lose the attachment to the things we perceive, we become more centered, as if in a state of light meditation. *IT* told Hermes that "Ultimately, you all return to the Light...The Light is a path you choose each moment" (The Hermetica 101, p. 52). This means that at some point, in some lifetime, all of us will awaken. Will you consciously choose to do so in this lifetime? Will you choose the path of the Happiness Warrior to awaken to your True-Self?

Re-Programming Our Conscious Mind

In the last chapter I have given a few examples of ways to achieve the varying levels of consciousness. We have learned that Lake-Thom encourages us to study each encounter with our external world using each part of our mind-brain complex. Don Juan taught how to let the spirit of a man flow and take over. Shamanic journeying allows us to work with the invisible worlds and formless energies. Monks and Mystics continuously integrate their inner and outer realities, while Hermes was taught to give up material attachments and to love unconditionally. All of these examples have one thing in common, comparing the external world with our inner world. 'Practice' becomes the bridge for us to experience these different levels of consciousness on a personal basis. I would like to express the importance of the concept 'believe it when you experience it'. I strongly encourage personal experiences to become your *ONLY* truth.

We have seen how every person has internal and external sources of knowledge, and how this knowledge has shaped our personality and our reactions. Taking the example of fire, we have been told (externally) that it is hot or we have fear (internally) that it can burn. On the opposite side, we have learned that ice is cold, but if we hold our hand in a bucket of ice water for long enough we will feel a burning sensation. The ice water is not on fire, yet it fools our brain into thinking it is. Here lies a conflict between the external and the internal. Our feelings are internal and we should grant them more influence over our decisions, rather than allowing our programmed mind to make decisions.

Let us now begin the process of acknowledging and trusting our divine side, or soul. This is possible through the use of affirmations. Affirmations work through re-training, or programming, the mind. We are subject to programming on a daily basis, but little of this programming is for our own good. The following are some examples of affirmations from Dr. Paul Leon Masters' *Ministers/Bachelors Degree Course*. Each affirmation should end in the words 'For this I give thanks and so it IS.' This adds a confirmation of your own belief in the statement. I encourage you to write your own affirmations. These can be written on a small piece of paper and carried around in your pocket so that you can repeat them several times a day.

"I radiate out auric vibrations of prosperity and well-being, wherever I may be each day." (p. 1: 15)

"Anything that appears to go wrong this day is immediately corrected and made right by the unseen Power of God working through me." (p. 1: 21)

"Every day, in every way, I am guided by my Higher God-Mind" (p. 1: 49)

Affirmations work by training our consciousness to focus on them. The information in the affirmations travels to the deeper levels of our consciousness every time we read or speak them. This is internal programming rather than external programming, of which both can cause random thoughts to pop into our heads. In his book *Beyond 2012-A Handbook for the New Area*, Wes Penre discusses how "few people are aware of how many thoughts are going through their heads every day" (p. 13). If every single thought was written down, even for a single day, the list would be surprisingly long. It would be noticeable that "… the majority of the thoughts we have in our heads are not our own, but thoughts we pick up from our environment" (p. 126). I would encourage everyone to write their own list, of their own thoughts and examine how many of them have been programmed through external sources. When we begin to become consciously aware of our thoughts, we begin to take control back, stop the thoughts running freely through our minds and increase the ability to make decisions from our True-Self rather than our environmental-Self. Maintaining an awareness of our thoughts, rids us of junk or sloppy thoughts, of which, Penre says, are followed up with similarly sloppy decisions.

Society has convinced humans into feeling more comfortable when someone else is in control, in other words when they are told what to do. The information in this book has provided an understanding that this has been the case since our parents' taught us manners and told us what and how to do things throughout childhood, then our school teachers, following on to our managers and even our partners. If we have always done what we were told, we had no opportunities to express creativity. When we are not creative and inspired, our peace of mind and happiness suffers. Penre emphasizes "this is why it's so important that you learn to analyze your thoughts and decisions" (Beyond 2012, p. 22), to become more content within yourself. It is much simpler than it seems, "practice being aware of what you're thinking and what you're saying so that what you express to yourself and others is what you want" (Beyond 2012,

p. 51). The aim is to recognize the difference between our True-Self and environmental-Selves' thoughts, and this in itself, will bring a sense of being present, increased focus, and improved mental stability (Beyond 2012, p. 126).

Penre, in another of his books, *A journey through the Multiverse*, says that "our thoughts and emotions are the two most powerful tools we have as human beings, and we need to use them wisely, for we get the reality we dream up..." (p. 531). Penre goes one step further expressing concerns about the numerous thoughts going through our heads and questions if we are even aware that movies and TV series contain subliminal frequencies transmitting messages convincing us that in order to survive we must "go-to-work, be silent and fearful" (p. 532). If this is the case it would add further weight to the fact that "...people are too caught up and involved in the functional insanity around them..." (p. 535). Becoming aware of our thoughts should move from a responsibility to an imperative part of daily living.

Dr. Masters' confirms the importance of analyzing our thoughts when he says "you must deliberately guard your conscious thinking" (Bachelor's Degree Curriculum, p. 1: 54). Looking into the history of

Western civilization shows how easily distracted, by external factors, we have become, but we must learn how to take responsibility of our thoughts. A strong motivation towards this responsibility is that these thoughts are happening within our own minds! If we don't take this task seriously, we are functioning in an auto-pilot manner where an emotional state of numbness and confusion resides. Dr. Masters regards "... every thought as a telepathic magnetic energy that can draw, or repel, good and happiness" (Bachelor's Degree Curriculum, p. 1: 56). If this is the case, negative thoughts bring negative situations, and therefore self-thought analysis becomes a worthwhile experiment for everyone.

In Eckhart Tolle's book, *The Power of Now: A Guide to Spiritual Enlightenment*, he states "those who have not found their true wealth, which is the radiant joy of Being and the deep, unshakable peace that comes with it, are beggars, even if they have great material wealth" (p. 12). This statement further confirms that no amount of wealth, or items of external form, will bring happiness and peace. Therefore to find an everlasting joy within ourselves, we must become conscious of our thinking. Tolle states that the greatest obstacle within life is the lack of "identification with your mind, which causes thought to become compulsive. Not to be able to stop thinking is a dreadful affliction, but we don't realize this because almost everybody is suffering from it, so it is considered normal" (p. 14). He describes uncontrolled thoughts as 'mental noise' which stops us from achieving inner peace, instead resulting in a sense of losing control leading to feelings of fear and suffering. Enlightenment, through thought analysis is a cure, providing a feeling of peace within, giving the confidence to embrace the life that unfolds before you. Tolle talks of mental noise as if it is a disease, which puts things out of balance and results in health issues.

We can become confused about how we use our mind, it is not limited to solving puzzles or fixing problems, we also have the ability to use our mind to become aware of our thoughts. "The moment you start watching the thinker, a higher level of consciousness becomes activated [it becomes realized] the things that truly matter [are]- beauty, love, creativity, joy, inner peace [of which] arise from beyond the mind" (The Power of Now, p. 17). We become free from the 'mental noise' by consciously becoming aware of our own thoughts. Tolle goes on to say that the majority of "people's thinking is not only repetitive and useless, but of its dysfunctional and often negative nature, much of it is also harmful" (The Power of Now, p. 22). Wasting energy on useless and negative thoughts drains our vital energy, leaving feelings of lethargy, restlessness and irritability. Tolle begins to then discuss the difference between the mind and the body:

> *"If you really want to know your mind, the body will always give you a truthful reflection, so look at the emotion, or rather feel it in your body. If there is an apparent conflict between them, the thought will be the lie, the emotion will be the truth. Not the ultimate truth of who you are, but the relative truth of your state of mind at that time"*

(The Power of Now, p. 26).

The ability of observing thoughts is equally as valuable as observing emotions. We can all relate to how the mind can run rampant with junk thoughts and it is comforting to know that the body attempts to bring us back towards our True-Self through our emotions. Whether they are thoughts or emotions, the focus should be on the observation on them. When one gains the ability to observe, one can distance the connection with the thought or emotion and therefore raise the consciousness above it, as opposed to becoming a slave to it. This process brings peace within through emotional detachment, and can be compared to watching a movie. When the detachment is achieved, a sense of mental composure occurs and it is realized that there is a choice in our reaction. With a clear head, the decision can be made to react with one's True-Self rather than the environmental-Self.

"Until you know what the mind is doing you cannot control it" (Vivekananda, p. 215). In order to become successful in life, become aware of your own thoughts and peace will result. Learning how to watch our own thoughts is like learning how to ride a bicycle. Once you have achieved it, you don't need to learn it again. If you haven't ridden for a while, it might take a little bit of effort to become fully confident as the process of trust, to balance on two wheels, has already been achieved. Those within Western Civilization should be aware of the conditioning that has taken place throughout life, so the process of learning to trust your True-Self is going to take patience and practice. With riding a bike, you must first gain the confidence towards trusting your body to balance itself when you take your feet off the ground. The mental and physical effort required to go from walking on two legs to having faith in two wheels often ends up with a few mishaps. No one can go through this process for you; it is only the determination within that will overcome the frustrations involved. Daily affirmations will help re-program the deeper levels of consciousness.

As our thoughts are continuously subject to external and internal influences, it is important to understand how this process works. Carl Jung, a prominent psychologist, simplified the levels of consciousness into three parts, the conscious mind, sub-conscious mind, and super-conscious mind. He refers to the super-conscious mind as the *Collective Unconscious*. The collective unconscious can be compared to a super-library where the information from humans, plants, animals, etc. is stored. Very few people have access to the super-conscious mind as it is so full of information that it would be difficult to comprehend. The conscious mind is a wonderful area to start, it is easy to access and observe. What are you thinking right now? It is that simple, but the power and influence it has is immense. For example, when we think of the word 'hot' it is generally associated with the color red. But fire burns at many different colors depending on temperature and what is burning. Where did we pick up the association of the word 'hot' and the color red? When we begin to consciously question what we have been told to be the truth, we engage our conscious mind. This exercise of questioning anything and everything works our consciousness and therefore strengthens it.

The conscious mind is active when we are not engaged in repetitive tasks. When an affirmation is read, either aloud or silently, it is subject to our conscious mind. When we attach emotions to our conscious thoughts they are fast tracked to our sub-conscious mind. Our subconscious mind can be compared to a personal library where all our thoughts and experiences are stored. Subconscious thoughts pop into our minds throughout the day and can have influence over our conscious thinking. This can be compared to sleep walking through our personal library and picking up a book and reading a chapter. We are generally unaware of the reason our subconscious thoughts are transferred to our conscious mind and therefore we are unprepared when they come through. For example, a song pops into your head, or you begin thinking of a past event while driving to work. These subconscious thoughts are fed from two different sources. Firstly, everything we hear, see, taste, touch and smell acts as an electrical/chemical stimulus which has the potential to create a thought, judgement or reaction. Therefore all this information can potentially become a subconscious memory. Our True-Self can also feed our subconscious mind. When we meditate we allow the

147

gates to open for thoughts or guidance to pass from our True-Self to our subconscious mind. These thoughts can sit in our subconscious until they eventually surface in our conscious mind.

Meditation

Not everyone is aware of the benefits to health and happiness that can be gained through the practice of meditation. Comparable to many individuals, my previous attempts at practicing meditation only left me feeling frustrated, anxious, and stressed due to an inability to rid my mind of all thoughts. Even the purchase of numerous meditation CD's were unable to propel me into a meditative state in order to heal my mind and body.

My metaphysical studies, from the very start, were urging meditation practice. With my unsuccessful history of attempts at meditating, I instantly felt a sense of failure. I decided to start with Dr. Masters book, *Meditation Dynamics*, which encouraged 5 minutes per day increasing up to 1 hour sessions per day. Starting with such a short time period didn't seem as daunting and I began practicing some of the exercises. The first exercise was to stare at a lit candle placed at eye level

(p. 13), although it didn't seem to work as I didn't feel any different. For some reason, this time, I didn't get frustrated as the book gave numerous different examples of how to achieve meditative states and encouraged trying a few out before giving up. After two weeks of practice, I found myself reclining in a chair with my eyes shut, quieting my mind. The next thing I notice is that I had become aware that my mind was free of thoughts. I felt distant from my own body, as if I was floating in a dark void. There was no light or sound, no feeling of gravity or heaviness, no stress, no anxiety, just a comfortable feeling of floating where I could experience peace and safety. This feeling was immediately followed by an intense belief of at last finding the home I had been searching for my whole life. It was as though I was being embraced by something and all I could think was "I have finally found home!" I opened my eyes and was overwhelmed with emotions which filled me with blissful energy. I had a realization that this home, this safety, that I had been searching for, was not something external to me, but internal. Immediately I grabbed my notepad and wrote the following:

I have found a home within me. I have found it in my connection to a Higher Source. This is the home I have been searching for my whole life. Even as a child I was aware of a dark hole, an empty space, trying to consume me. I could feel this darkness when I had my breakfast, it felt like an overwhelming sadness that sometimes brought tears to my eyes for no apparent reason. Some nights, when in bed, I would shut my eyes and experience the same feeling of falling into a never ending black hole. I used to force my eyes to open in order to shake this feeling off before I could go to sleep. This hole has come to an end because I now realize that this is the lifetime where I am going to release all of my negative vibrations.

From that point onwards, I have been practicing meditation on a daily basis and have learned how to achieve light meditational states throughout my daily activities. My clarity improved, my health has improved, as has my success and happiness. I am aware when I achieve higher states of consciousness and due to this, have flashes of inspiration throughout the day. My intuitive senses allow me to pick up on knowledge not previously known to me and I confidently follow higher guidance with faith and trust. The majority of my days are filled with extremely high energy levels, while the remaining days I don't feel guilty when resting.

Meditation can bring anyone a greater appreciation of the world around us, enabling us to increase the ability of our senses, and even awaken dormant senses. Marsha Sinetar says "what is necessary and highly practical is to create simple routines and structure in our lives so that we can meditate, reflect, sit in quiet and thus grow from this understanding" (p. 150).

Meditation is like any other skill, it needs to be practiced. Unfortunately we have been taught that meditation involves sitting on the top of a mountain in a cross legged position for hours upon end, where all thought is emptied and our senses are completely cut off. This, when attempted by most, is an incomprehensible practice. For some reason, a person who has never meditated before puts pressure on themselves to find the same peaceful state of mind that the person sitting on top of the mountain has. Meditation is a skill that has to be learned, like any other skill. Sinetar says that "straining the mind blank turns people away from meditation" (p. 152), instead they should be enjoying the natural ebb and flow of life, which is much like meditation and is achieved by taking more time to reflect and "walk about in the beauty of nature" (p. 151).

When we begin to appreciate the world around us, notice it and notice how it makes us feel, we *ARE* in a light state of meditation. One aim of "meditative experiences ought to be such that we discover our strengths and weaknesses and come to terms with ourselves nonjudgmentally" (Sinetar, p. 153). Sinetar describes meditation as alleviating "certain physical stresses, enabling one to feel more gratified, safer, less anxious, less despairing. In its ultimate form, a meditation program may enable us to reap the fruits of our fullest humanity, whether we call this enlightenment, actualization, Being or Selfhood" (Sinetar, p. 164). Through meditation we can improve our ability to consciously become aware of the thoughts that pass through our mind, impartially, as opposed to dwelling on those thoughts (Sinetar, p. 165), bringing our "attention to deeper, more subtle levels of being" (Sinetar, p. 166). In this light state of meditation we can then observe in a controlled manner, avoiding suppression of emotions, which drains creative potential and weakens our character. Meditation, of which there are many forms, is "capable of lowering stress and enhancing health... [and gives us the ability to observe, rather than partake, in the]... never-ending action and antics of the restless mind" (Sinetar, p. 167). Sinetar states the process to becoming whole is to firstly be willing to "*look* at ourselves honestly... [and have] the humility to acknowledge that we are imperfect" (p. 171).

It can now be understood that watching our thoughts is a form of achieving light meditational states. Therefore anyone who can listen to their own thinking can meditate!

Thought Processing and Emotions

Being aware of our thoughts and meditation are both forms of consciously processing the information we receive. Our mental and physical health depends on processing the information we receive. Dr. Masters understood that "an Inner Intelligence is regulating the dream content that is taking place on an unconscious level" (Masters Degree Modules, p. 2: 38). In this way our dreams are actively processing information as well as communicating with the deeper levels of our Pure Mind. This unconscious processing is happening automatically, when we sleep. Humans utilise this processing ability and subsequently this skill can be increased during waking hours.

Some people remember their dreams and can describe the visual pictures seen within them. But these pictures are not generated through our eyes, rather they are purely electrical/chemical signals interpreted by our brains as visual images. Joyce Schenkein, a neuropsychologist, refers to a study by A. Valvo in 1971, in her article "Why Can We See Things in Our Dreams When Our Eyes Are Closed". This study involved a number of people whom, due to accidents, had lost their sight. Throughout the next twenty years, their dreams became more tactile and auditory compared to a person with sight who dreams in visual images. As our sensory input changes, our brain adapts affecting our conscious and unconscious awareness. "After twenty years of blindness, the subjects...underwent a new surgical procedure to restore the optics [connected to] their eyes" (Schenkein, p. n.p.). Only one subject, who throughout the twenty years, continued to use his imagination to visualize what he touched, regained his sight. His belief in what he was visualizing, in his imagination, kept his brain actively wired. The other subjects, whom never exercised any visual processing through their imagination, lost this ability. This study "reported that patients with Parietal lobe damage could not construct the stage upon which the visual dream occurs" (Schenkein, p. n.p. qtd.). This part of the brain understands space and direction and when not utilized, looses the ability to visualize in dreams. Those born blind do not set up their visual brain and therefore are unable to dream in pictures. In this way, our senses have an impact on the content of our dreams. Our ability to process large amounts of detailed information is available and when exercised this amount can be increased. In other words, our system adapts to support what is required for us to function. Through our own eyes we think we can see the whole scale of vision and in that belief we are limiting ourselves. We understand that many animals can see better in the dark although if we were to spend the majority of our time in the dark, exercising our eyes in the lack of light, we would become better adjusted to it.

It has been discussed that the electrical signals travelling through our system hold information on the number of stimuli and their intensities. We also understand that love is an emotion, from deeper levels, which also accompanies these electrical signals. Not all emotions are based from the depths our Pure Mind; some have been acquired through our environment and therefore part of our egoic mind. Rebecca Rago says that "beyond our perception, our senses play an integral role in our emotional processing, learning and interpretation" (p. n.p.). For example, when most people stand on the edge of a cliff they experience the emotion of fear. Their eyes sense the distance to the bottom of the cliff and calculate the possibility of survival if the body were to fall. With the body at risk of survival, the brain reacts by inducing fear, causing the body to freeze in place or back away from the edge. In this case fear is the emotion which has attached itself to the sensory information of viewing a dangerous situation. Because the eyes saw the cliff, the emotion of fear has been generated from our environment. This is different to the emotion of love which is not a product of our environment, but instead comes from the depths within.

As sensory information comes from a different source than emotional information, is it possible to relate both sources on a spiritual level? In *The Hermetica 101*, Matthew Barnes translates that the Mind of God created the Cosmos and the Universe and that "within this world the One became Two – a male and a female part, a positive and a negative pole...the yang and yin, the proton and electron" (p. 83). The two opposite, positive and negative energies, are in constant movement which generate our "Life Force" (p. 84). This Life Force is energy which is contained within every cell, organ, muscle and tissue within us. It is also contained within everything external to us as well as everything within the Cosmos, albeit on a larger scale. In this way Life Force, emotions, and sensory stimuli are all forms of energy. As we process these energies, our environmental-Self and spiritual-Self have a part in deciding which emotional charge becomes attached to the stimulus. The next time that stimulus is sensed the very same emotional charge will attach itself through a type of memory association. "...Like everything else we feel about the world, they are memories we accumulate. Memories of the description" (Castaneda, p. 51). When we question the descriptive emotion that attaches itself to the stimulus, instead of just allowing it, we break the memory cycle. In other words, when we question the foundation of our own judgments, feelings, or emotions, we move away from limiting ourselves to one part of the mind. If we then refuse to attach any initial negative emotional charge to a stimulus, we strengthen the connection to our divine-Self and its guidance.

Our emotional links to the sense of taste have a lot to teach us. The terms 'home cooking' or 'just like mama used to make it' are well known and a way we relate taste with previous memories. As children we are more open to the wonders of the world, our imagination runs wild and we spend time with our friends for hours on end. During that time we may have participated in energetic, playful, activities and probably built up quite an appetite through running and racing around. After such an exciting day, we may have returned home to find a hot meal waiting to be served. We were told to wash up before sitting down to eat. This meal is appreciated, more so, after having worked up an appetite through positive activities. Is this why 'home cooking' always holds a special place in our hearts? Does this mean our appreciation of things can be impacted by the environment around us or our emotional state? Yes. These emotional links can also be experienced by adults. For example, you may enjoy a bottle of wine on holiday and decide to bring it home. For some reason it never tastes the same at home. The phrase 'it doesn't travel well', suggests that other people have experienced the same thing. Is the reasoning behind this due to the difference in the temperature of the wine or the climate when on holiday? Or is it down to the fact that on holiday, you were relaxed and care free, with no deadlines or structure, and therefore able to enjoy it more?

Finding Strength to Grow

Through my research and practice I have realized that everything around us has the same origin, the same spirit of divineness within it. "Seek and see the marvels all around you. You'll get tired of looking at yourself alone, and that fatigue will make you deaf and blind to everything else" (The Teachings of Don Juan, p. 19). This quote suggests that when we open our hearts to our environment and appreciate everything for what it is, we view everything in the Light of Love. This Light will diminish our negative judgments and replace them with the appreciation of all that life has to offer. This foundation will provide a "calmness of mind [which] does not mean you should stop your activity. [As] real calmness should [and can] be found in activity itself" (Dass, p. 138, qtd.).

We are all grains of sand on the beach, without each individual grain, there would be no beach. Each of us has a part in this Universe and that part begins as an individual one which allows the Universal system to function as a whole. Without our individual aspects there would be no functioning system. Instead of following in others ideas or instructions, we should be using our individual aspects, our creativeness, which are qualities given to us at birth and releasing those abilities into the world to help its evolvement as well as our own. If we continue to live by other's views, we lose our True-Self and become the follower of others. When we are creative and expressive, we are embracing life itself.

Mystics use every opportunity as one of growth while the majority of humanity seem to be more comfortable following in others footsteps, without evolving. When we understand that every life situation has something to teach us about ourselves and others, it takes the sting out of difficult experiences. This is because there is faith in the knowledge that in the end, the main goal is one of learning. The more we become aware of what is around us, the more we appreciate our surroundings and the more we appreciate ourselves.

"Creative or inspired thought that can bring success and prosperity originates as a deeper level of mind than one's conscious intellect" (Masters P. L., Bachelor's Degree Curriculum, p. 2: 62). Everything that has brought us our favourite memories have been a result of actions from our instinctive or True-Self, while everything else of a negative nature has been a result of actions from our environmental-Self.

Although it may be perceived that others live the perfect life, no individual can admit that they are perfect in every way. Perfection should be a practice of continuous improvements. Alan Watts is a British philosopher and supporter of Eastern philosophy, who lectured "…when dancing you don't aim at a particular spot in the room, that is where you should arrive. The whole point of the dancing is the dance. Now, but we don't see that." (Watts, 2017). The ability to take joy in everything we do, every part or our journey, has been lost and replaced with delaying joy until we have accomplished, purchased, or completed, something.

Life is available to us for living. If every moment is not cherished then you need to ask yourself the question 'am I living my life to its full potential?' As far as your individual purpose in life, the answers lie within you, all you need to do is ask your True-Self the question.

We should restrict outside factors governing how we feel inside. In order to find one's Higher-Self, Dr. Masters states that one must integrate an awareness of their thoughts "…into conscious daily life…" (Bachelor's Degree Curriculum, p. 2: 20). This practice is a form of Metaphysical Science analysis and it "…can help stimulate insight and intuition…," (Bachelor's Degree Curriculum, p. 2: 28) which is generated from one's Higher-Self. Constant questioning of every thought that enters our mind will allow us to decipher if its energy is positive or negative. Our Higher-Self will generate excitement as it fills our bodies with positive vibrational energies, while our environmental-Self will do the opposite. We should be continually asking ourselves if a thought has come from our external situation, entered the mind through other peoples' opinions, or their experiences of the world around them (Bachelor's Degree Curriculum, p. 2: 46). To understand this will be of great benefit when it comes to reaching a conclusion as to the external or internal foundation of the thought. This process will enable one to become more aware of instinctive thoughts and react with more control and confidence in life. The more we to learn to rely on our Higher-Self, the more enriching life becomes. Learn to rely on your instinct rather than your intellect and analytical deduction (Bachelor's Degree Curriculum, p. 2: 48).

Are there any ways we can increase our confidence in the acknowledgment and examination of our thoughts, emotions and sensory input? Sometimes confidence can be boosted by encouragement from others, as in the case of a young boy at school. "Years ago a teacher in Detroit asked Stevie Morris to help her find a mouse that was lost in the classroom...she appreciated the fact that nature had given Stevie something no one else in the room had. Nature had given Stevie a remarkable pair of ears to compensate for his blind eyes" (Carnegie, p. 45). This appreciation of Stevie's heightened sense of hearing did two things; it showed the other children in the class that Stevie had hearing abilities beyond their own and they forgot about teasing him due to his blindness. By finding the mouse he became the classroom hero, which in turn, gave him the confidence to further develop his hearing into adulthood. He became a famous pop singer, eventually adopting the stage name of Stevie Wonder.

Confidence is not only gained through support from others, it can also be gained through practicing a skill or personal experience. When we turn our focus inwards, to the deeper levels of our mind, we can find the confidence to increase our own abilities. If we wait for someone else to give us the confidence, we may never achieve it. Monks, mystics, shamans, Native American Indians, and those who meditate, are continually working towards building their own confidence, from within. These are all *normal* people who persistently make the decision to allocate time to look at and observe Nature, the Earth, the Cosmos and deep within themselves.

Gaining confidence through practice is possible as the more a skill is practiced, the more proficient we become at it. In the article "The amazing Phenomenon of Muscle Memory" by Ainsile Johnstone, she discusses that "everyday actions involve a complex sequence of tensing and relaxing many different muscles" (p. n.p.). When these actions are repeated over time, they become faster and more accurate until eventually they "can be preformed almost automatically and without thought" (p. n.p.). Many repetitive actions result in the strengthening of active muscles and in order to compensate for this the brain is continually adapting the information sent to each muscle. In this way the brain is accumulating muscle memory, as well as making adjustments for muscle strength increases. Johnstone proves an increase in hand-eye coordination in subjects that spent six weeks training to juggle. The study showed that there was an increase in "white matter connections between regions of the brain responsible for vision and regions responsible for making movements...[The] increased connections between [the] visual and movement [regions of the brain] resulted in faster and easier sharing of information" (p. n.p.). In other words, when we use our muscles to practice any skill, we improve our abilities due to our brain becoming more efficient at adapting to the transfer of information. Therefore when we practice becoming aware of the information our senses pick up, we can subsequently gain the skill of becoming aware of the emotions we attach to that information. The more this is practiced, the quicker and more automatic it becomes until eventually the skill requires no conscious effort.

To achieve light states of meditation it really is as simple as examining our emotions and thoughts while detaching ourselves from our initial judgment, therefore gaining the ability to control the resultant thought or response. This skill will bring us closer to the depths of our mind allowing us to raise our own consciousness above the auto-pilot mode of living. A consciously aware frame of mind brings clarity and encourages the questioning of everything to find how things affect us on a personal level. Being inquisitive in this way brings a new level of understanding where "...the world we think we see is only a view, a description of the world. [In order to comprehend this]...seems to be one of the hardest things one can do; we are complacently caught in our particular view of the world, which compels us to feel and act as if we knew everything about this world" (Castaneda, p. 229).

If for a moment, we stop making judgments from our environmental-Self we can begin to see things for what they really are. For example, while driving, someone may recklessly overtake and brake suddenly causing us to take action in order to avoid an accident. What if we were unaware of their reasoning behind their actions? What if it became known that the drivers' child had started choking in the passenger seat and that the reckless driving was due to the parent panicking about dislodging the obstruction in their child's throat. When a parent panics in an attempt to save their child's life, other road users' safety becomes secondary in priority. If it was known that a child's life was at risk, our own initial reaction to the reckless driving would have been different. When we stop judging we stop making incorrect assumptions. This is an imperative step in tipping the balance away from our rational thinking and moving it towards our intuition, allowing our responses to be based from our True-Self. "One can arrive at the totality of oneself only when one fully understands that the world is merely a view..." (Castaneda, p. 238). The view we have of the world is from one perspective, we need to broaden our thinking and become more intuitive in the situations we face.

"The secret of all this is one's attention...All of this exists only because of our attention. This very rock we're sitting on is a rock because we have been forced to give our attention to it as a rock" (Castaneda, p. 232). When we examine the reality around us, our attention becomes focused on observation. Our surroundings are acknowledged through the stimulus our senses receive and that information is then processed into a different form. The information, en-route to the brain, is susceptible to rational judgments or over-analysis in our environmental-Self's attempt to find a solution. But only part of our mind is rational which thrives on judgmental thoughts and finding solutions. When our awareness is trained to accept the reality around us, we begin to release the need to change our environment and become the observer, utilizing the depths of our non-rational mind. In this way we are heightening our sensitivities, moving towards the instinctive qualities of animals.

Groups of animals have social fields encompassing each individual where habitual patterns, formed throughout the generations, become collective habits or instincts. "Termite colonies, schools of fish, flocks of birds, herds, packs, and other animal groups are also held together and structured by morphic fields, and these fields are all shaped by their own kinds of collective memory" (*Sheldrake* 24). Instinctive abilities are transferred memories within the group which are not limited by time and space (*Sheldrake* 25). The information available within the deepest levels of our mind also transcends time and space. For mystics, this is their goal, to connect with the collective information. We have to be patient with ourselves in order to achieve this connection as it requires a change in perspective. "Wholeness does not arrive by our willing it...By relaxing our grip on an inordinate need for perfection, we create a richer emotional atmosphere of acceptance and experience a greater degree of integration" (Sinetar 145). The process to obtain these abilities is rarely instantaneous; instead it requires patience and practice.

Wild animals have a strong union with Nature and the Earth making direct connections with both just by living in it and travelling around on it. Our connection with Nature and the Earth is restricted by rubber soled shoes and further limited by spending a majority of our time within buildings or homes. The bulk of what we believe our senses to be capable of is governed by lessons we have been taught at school, what we watch on television, or read in newspapers. Anybody who has been involved in filming any program will be able to disclose that a large proportion of footage recorded does not actually make it into the final version. All the information we are given through the media is at the discretion of the editor, director, as well as the individual(s) funding it. Misrepresentation is widespread in the media and unfortunately, has a large impact on the way we think, how we react, and how our environmental-Self has evolved. Our senses have been contaminated and suppressed to the point we are more reliant on other peoples' opinions rather than our own, deep felt, understanding of the world around us. Animals don't pay attention to the news or distract themselves with the media and therefore their senses are not contaminated. Instead they survive by being more aware of what is actually around them, not what they are told is around them.

There is still hope for human beings as no "matter how urbanized the world becomes... [we] are still living in Nature" (Lake-Thom, p. 5). The fresh air we breathe, the uncontaminated water we drink, the unprocessed food we eat, all connect us to Nature and the Earth, although these connections are ungratefully received or even go unrecognized. With pollution increasing in built up cities, Nature continues to exist and is constantly communicating inside and outside our perceptions (Lake-Thom, p. 5). The communication is out there and available; we just need to retrain our ability to acknowledge, observe, be grateful for, and understand what it means to each of us personally.

Finding inner-peace requires determination, one must have faith in achieving it and the commitment to follow it through. Everybody has faith in something, even those who consider themselves non-religious. To put one's faith in their Higher-Self either requires a life threatening situation, to be forced into a corner from negative obstacles until we generate the inner power to change the situation, or through choice. If a decision is made to find inner-peace and the determination is there to follow the decision through then it will be so.

The questioning of our own thoughts will show us how our minds process the external and internal factors. We can then begin to move away from external thinking such as judging without knowing, desire without need, and self-destructive practices. As young children, racism had no meaning; external influences taught us how to stereotype humans. As babies we had no concerns with our body shape, society has taught us what body shapes are acceptable, but even that is not consistent as the ideal body figure changes throughout history. When we find ourselves having thoughts which are different to those which have been programmed, we must question where they came from. As Penre said, "we all need to be exceptionally clear in thought, in words and deed" (Penre, A Journey Through the Multiverse, p. 537).

If you are looking for an answer on how to find peace, it starts with discarding the rambling thoughts running through our minds. I cannot prescribe a pill to do such a thing as the process itself brings enlightenment. There is no sense of accomplishment from collecting a badge for running a marathon if you jumped in a car at the start and got out at the finish line. Your True-Self would not let you be satisfied with that. Every thought you catch is a step in the right direction. YOU do the work, YOU reap the benefits.

Our external influences have taught our ego to rely on the input of other people's view points, leading us into situations that we are not comfortable with. This is one way our instinctive-Self is trying to 'wake us up', by giving us clues that we are wasting our time and energies. A friend once told me that she was accused of stealing from her boss. She knew she was innocent, but had no way of proving this fact. Because of this situation, she held on to negative feelings for decades, which were mentally upsetting her, just as her boss had. Her True-Self always knew that she was wrongly accused, but she allowed her ego to continually cause her heartache. Why was it not possible to just accept, within herself, that she was in the right, her boss was mistaken, forgive their misguided reprimands, and grow from the situation? The power to trust in herself was overtaken by her ego's ability to punish with it's circling negative thoughts. She did not have the inner strength to free herself from her ego, or maybe she didn't realize that her ego was only part of her personality and not her True-Self. When did our ability to trust in ourselves get lost?

Scientific studies in the connection of emotions to stimulus are at their infancy because the connection lies in one of personal growth and personal experience. Everybody experiences things differently. An ant can look at a blade of grass as we would look at a high rise building. Everything is relative and everything has a personal importance. God created everything so that it could have its own experience. The contamination occurs when we are forced to take on the experiences of others and become tricked into thinking it is the truth. If we were meant to have the same perspective as every other human then we would have all been created the same. "The flaw with words…[is that] they always force us to feel enlightened, but when we turn around to face the world they always fail us and we end up facing the world as we always have, without enlightenment" (*Tales of Power* 29).

My words are only a means of motivation for you to find your own truth. Remember to view the world as if you are a child, soak up the knowledge it has to give and study the feelings it provides. Emotions are lessons from the soul as they come from the heart. If our emotions are adopted from others, they can be disregarded. If one person says you must try a particular type of food because it is amazing, try it. If your first reaction is from your heart, it will be your True-Self communicating with you. If you didn't like it but didn't want to hurt others feelings and said it was as good as they described, you have adopted another person's emotion. In this way you have now created an environmental-Self memory. "The moment you become aware of the ego in you, it is strictly speaking no longer the ego, but just an old conditioned mind-pattern. Ego implies unawareness. Awareness and ego cannot coexist" (*A New Earth* Ch.3).

Awareness should be focused on our own soul which has its own connections with a Higher Power. "If you open your heart to God in meditation, God's Heart will open itself to you, leaving you pure in mind, to feel worthy of any of life's riches" (*Ministers/Bachelor's Degree Modules* 4: 66). When we open ourselves to others and show our True-Self, we form stronger bonds with them. This is why our relationships with animals are often stronger than those with our own families and friends, because there is no involvement from our ego.

Forming a relationship with our instinctive, True-Self brings confidence, strength, and positive guidance. At first this relationship can be confusing. Don Juan describes the *nagual* as being beyond our comprehension, a power that sits outside of our awareness which has infinite abilities. Our soul can communicate with the *nagual* in a way that we begin to notice "on certain occasions… or under certain special circumstances, something in the *tonal* [our awareness] itself becomes aware that there is more to us. It is like a voice that comes from the depths" (*Tales of Power* 131).

In closing I give you a Daruma good luck doll. Make a wish to connect with your True-Self and draw a black pupil in one of its eyes. When your wish comes true, come back to this book and fill in the second eye.

Many blessings

Figure 10. Daruma Good Luck Doll

Works Cited

(US), O. o. (2001, August). The Influence of Culture and Society on Mental Health. (Chapter 2 Culture Counts:). Retrieved January 6, 2020, from https://www.ncbi.nlm.nih.gov/books/NBK44249/

Advertising Archives. (n.d.). Retrieved September 2, 2020, from https://www.advertisingarchives.co.uk/.

Alexander, G. (2016). The Civilization of Fear. *Journal of Political Sciences & Public Afairs*, Volume 4 Issue 3 1000219. doi:10.4172/2332-D761.1000219

Barnes, M. (2016). *The Hermetica 101*. USA: Matthew S. Barnes.

Barnes, M. S. (2016). *The Emerald Tablet 101*. United States of America: Matthew S. Barnes.

Barrows, L. C. (2106). Andrew Tragowski, Western Civilization in the 21st Century. *Comparative Civilizations Review, 74:No.74, Article 10*.

Works Cited

Bates, M. (2012, September 18). *ScientificAmerican.com*. Retrieved January 24, 2020

Burger, N. (Director). (2011). *Limitless* [Motion Picture]. New York City: Universal Pictures UK. Retrieved 2014

Cantril, H. (1940). *The Invasion From Mars: A Study in the Psychology of Panic*. New Jersey, USA: Princeton University Press.

Carnegie, D. (1981). *How to Win Friends and Influence People*. New York, New York: Simon and Schuster Publishing.

Castaneda, C. (1974). *Tales of Power*. New York, New York: Penguin Books.

Castaneda, C. (1986). *The Teachings of Don Juan: A Yaqui Way of Knowledge*. CA: University of California Press.

Christian, B. (2017, August 7). Retrieved February 14, 2020, from www.wired.co.uk.

Dass, R. (1978). *Journey of Awakening*. New York: Bantam Books.

Dictionary, C. (n.d.). "Sense" definition. Retrieved February 2, 2020, from www.dictionary.cambridge.org

Ferguson, N. (2011). *Civilization: The West and the Rest*. London, England: Penguin Group.

Fuller, H. Q. (1978). *Physics: Including Human Applications*. New York: Harper & Row.

General, O. o. (2001, August). The Influence of Culture and Society on Mental Health. (Chapter 2 Culture Counts:). United States. Retrieved January 6, 2020, from https://www.ncbi.nlm.nih.gov/books/NBK44249/

Hindle, C. (2016, November 17). *10 Levels of Consciousness – Which One Are You At?* Retrieved October 1, 2020, from Learning Mind: https://www.learning-mind.com/10-levels-of-consciousness/

Ingerman, S. (2014). *Walking In Light: the Everyday Empowerment of a Shamanic Life*. Boulder, CO.: Sounds True Publishing.

Johnstone, A. (2017, December 14). *The Amazing Phenomenon of Muscle Memory*. Retrieved February 7, 2020, from Medium.com: www.medium.com/oxford-university

Jung, C. (1959). *The Archetypes and the Collective Unconscious*. England: Routledge & Kegan Paul Ltd.

Lake-Thom, B. (1997). *Spirits of the Earth*. New York: Penguin Group.

Works Cited

MacDonald, F. (2016, October 26). *An English-Speaking Teenager Has Woken Up From a Coma Speaking Fluent Spanish.* Retrieved February 3, 2020, from www.sciencealert.com.

Marilyn Mendoza, P., & Mendoza, M. (2018, March 12). Retrieved February 4, 2020, from PsychologyToday.com.

Marr, A. (2012). *A History of the World.* London, England: Macmillian Publishers Ltd.

Masters, P. L. (2012). *Masters Degree Modules.* Sedona, AZ: University of Sedona Publishing.

Masters, P. L. (2012). *Master's Degree Modules.* Sedona, Arizona: University of Sedona Publishing.

Masters, P. L. (2012). *Ministers/Bachelor's Degree Curriculum.* Sedona, AZ: University of Sedona Publishing.

Masters, P. L. (2016). *Meditation Dynamics.* Sedona, AZ: International Metaphysical Ministry.

Neal, M. (2016, January 18). *Is Watching TV Actually A Good Way to Rest Your Brain?* Retrieved December 20, 2019, from Vice.com.

Penre, W. (1998, November 12). The Wes Penre Papers: Introductory Level of Learning. http://illuminati-news.com/moriah.htm.

Penre, W. (2011). The Wes Penre Papers – A journey through the Multiverse (First Level of Learning).

Penre, W. (2013). *Beyond 2012 – A Handbook for the New Area*. Wes Penre Productions.

Rago, R. (2014, October 9). *Emotion and Our Senses*. Retrieved January 25, 2020, from Tufts Wordpress Blogs and Websites: https://sites.tufts.edu/emotiononthebrain/2014/10/09/emotion-and-our-senses/

Redfield, J., & Adrienne, C. (1995). *The Celestine Prophecy: An Experimental Guide*. London, Great Britian: Bantam Books.

Schenkein, J. (n.d.). *Why Can We See Things In Our Dreams When Our Eyes Are Closed*. Retrieved February 2, 2020, from www.forbes.com.

Sheldrake, R. (1999). *Dogs That Know When Their Owners Are Coming Home and Other Unexplained Powers of Animals*. New York: Crown Publishers.

Works Cited

Sinetar, M. (1986). *Ordinary People as Monks & Mystics: Lifestyles for Spiritual Wholeness*. New Jersey: Paulist Press.

Tolle, E. (2004). *The Power Of Now: A Guide To Spiritual Enlightenment*. Australia: Hodder Australia.

Vivekananda, S. (2017). *The Four Paths of Yoga*. New York: Discovery Publisher.

Watts, A. (2017, September 6). Life is NOT a Journey. (A. Skool, Ed.) YouTube.com.

Willis, C. (2018). *The End from the Beginning: The Origin of Western Civilization*. Independently published.

Index

Table of Figures

About the Author

Clare Hinsley is a Doctor of Philosophy specializing in Metaphysical Counselling, earned through the University of Sedona, Arizona. She also holds a Bachelor and Masters degree in Metaphysical Science from the University of Metaphysics.

Dr. Hinsley is an Ordained Metaphysical Minister with the ability to heal individuals and instil them with the confidence to deal with everyday life situations as they occur. Working with the positive spiritual energies, Dr. Hinsley achieves a pure, non-medicated, approach to healing addressing the root cause of the issue.

Her interests lie in philosophies and practices from Eastern, Native American, Shamanic, ancient Egyptian, and Western origins.

Born in the UK, most of her childhood was spent in California before returning to the UK where she now currently resides in Wiltshire.

Dr. Hinsley is eager to promote the incredible benefits of Metaphysics. For more information, please see her website http://loosh.co.uk.